DIFFERENTIAL DIAGNOSIS IN AIDS
– A Color Guide

J.M. Parkin
MB, BS, MRCP, PhD
Senior Registrar in Immunology
St Mary's Hospital,
London

B.S. Peters
MB, BS, MRCP
Registrar in Immunology and Infectious Disease
St Mary's Hospital,
London

Mosby
Year Book

St. Louis   Baltimore   Boston   Chicago   London   Philadelphia   Sydney   Toronto

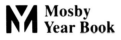

**Mosby
Year Book**

Dedicated to Publishing Excellence

Mosby–Year Book, Inc.
11830 Westline Drive
St. Louis, MO 63146

ISBN 0-8151-4434-6

English edition first published by Wolfe Publishing Ltd,
2–16 Torrington Place, London WC1E 7LT, UK.

Library of Congress Cataloging in Publication Data has been applied for

PREFACE

The number of individuals with HIV-related disease continues to rise. These patients do not always fall conveniently into the well-recognised risk groups for HIV infection, or attend centres specialising in the disease. Therefore, all clinicians need to be aware of the ways in which HIV may present.

The symptoms and signs of HIV-related disease are diverse. The progressive immune deficiency leads to the characteristic presentation of AIDS patients with overwhelming opportunist infections caused by usually non-pathogenic organisms, such as *Pneumocystis carinii*, and opportunist tumours, notably Kaposi's sarcoma. However, 'opportunist' infection may also be due to pathogens well-known to cause disease in the immunologically intact host, such as *Mycobacterium tuberculosis*, the infections presenting atypically, or being unusually severe in the immunosuppressed AIDS patient. Multiple infections are frequent, and infections contracted many years previously may re-emerge, only leaving their dormant state as the immune deficiency unfolds. The individual's microbiological environment, past and present, will therefore determine the infections which develop. Many of the minor infections observed are also common in the non-HIV-infected population, but have prognostic significance in those who are HIV-positive, and diagnosis is therefore important. Direct infection of the nervous system by HIV is another important manifestation of this organism, and some patients may present with marked neurological disease in the absence of severe immune deficiency.

The impairment of the immune system means that the basis for diagnosis of infection is often different to that in the immunocompetent person. Loss of the T-lymphocyte regulation of memory B-cells results in raised levels of antibody to previously encountered antigens. However, there is an inability to respond to new antigenic challenges. Therefore, the presence of a specific antibody will be of use in determining past exposure to infectious agents, some of which have the potential to reactivate, but it is generally unhelpful in the diagnosis of acute infection, as IgM or increasing antibody titres may not be detectable.

Clinical skills in combination with the selection of appropriate diagnostic tests, often involving direct tissue diagnosis, are paramount if these patients are to be managed optimally. The reward of early diagnosis and treatment, along with the use of specific anti-HIV agents, is prolonged survival and improved quality of life of individuals with HIV infection.

The aim of this atlas is to illustrate the problem-solving process in known HIV-infected patients presenting with suspected infection or tumour, together with the conditions that alert the clinician to the presence of HIV-related disease and, conversely, to those that may be mistaken for HIV-related conditions. The vast majority of patients presented have been under our care and therefore represent 'real-life' cases. Most of the differential diagnoses given for each case are of HIV-related conditions, but we have also mentioned or even illustrated non-HIV-associated conditions where appropriate.

J.M. PARKIN
B.S. PETERS
1991

ACKNOWLEDGEMENTS

We would like to thank our colleagues for encouragement in this project, especially Dr Anthony Pinching, who has given helpful comments on the text and provided some of the clinical slides; and two of the specialist contributors, Dr Moira McCarty and Dr Nick Francis, for providing most of the radiology and histopathology slides respectively, and for advice on their interpretation. In addition, we are grateful to other colleagues for allowing us to present their material: in particular, Professor J. Weber, Dr J. Leonard, Dr J.R.W. Harris, Dr C. Conlon, Mr R. Marsh, Mr M. Savage, Dr M. Helbert, Dr J. Cohen, Dr J. Howes, Dr R. Logan, Dr R. Goldin, Dr M. O'Docherty, Mr C. Clark, Dr C. Taylor and Dr R. Shaw; and the audiovisual departments at St Mary's Hospital and the Western Ophthalmic Hospital for their excellent reproductions and their help with this project.

Dedication
To the patients, past and present

Centre for Disease Control (CDC) Classification of HIV Infection

Group 1 Acute infection

Group 2 Asymptomatic infection

Group 3 Persistent generalised lymphadenopathy

Group 4 A. Constitutional disease

B. Neurological disease

C. Secondary infectious disease:–

Category C1 – Specified secondary infections listed in the CDC criteria for AIDS.

Category C2 – Other specified secondary infectious diseases.

D. Secondary cancers

E. Other conditions.

Indicator Diseases for Diagnosis of AIDS

Indicator Diseases for the Diagnosis of AIDS (CDC Group 4, adapted from MMWR 1987, Vol 36)

The following conditions can be used as indicator diseases for AIDS even if the HIV status of the patient is unknown, providing other causes of immune deficiency have been excluded (congenital immune deficiency, lymphoma/leukaemia, recent use of steroids or other immunosuppressive drugs).

- Candidiasis affecting the oesophagus, trachea, bronchi or lungs.
- Extrapulmonary cryptococcosis.
- Cryptosporidiosis with diarrhoea persisting for greater than one month.
- Cytomegalovirus infection, other than liver, spleen or lymph node, in a patient greater than one month of age.
- Herpes simplex causing a mucocutaneous ulcer for greater than one month, or bronchitis, pneumonitis or oesophagitis for any duration in a patient greater than one month of age.
- Kaposi's sarcoma in a patient less than 60 years of age.
- Primary lymphoma of the brain in a patient less than 60 years of age.
- Lymphoid interstitial pneumonitis or pulmonary lymphoid hyperplasia in a child less than 13 years of age.
- *Mycobacterium avium* complex or *M. kansasii* infection with disseminated disease (other than, or in addition to, lungs, skin, cervical or hilar lymph nodes).
- *Pneumocystis carinii* pneumonia.
- Progressive multifocal leukoencephalopathy.
- Cerebral toxoplasmosis in a patient greater than one month of age.

The following are indicator diseases for diagnosis of AIDS *only if there is also evidence of HIV infection:*

- Disseminated coccidioidomycosis or histoplasmosis.
- HIV encephalopathy.
- Isosporiasis with diarrhoea persisting for greater than one month.
- Kaposi's sarcoma at any age.
- Primary lymphoma of the brain at any age.
- Other non-Hodgkin's lymphoma, of B-cell or unknown phenotype.
- Extrapulmonary tuberculosis.
- Salmonella septicaemia, recurrent.
- HIV wasting syndrome.

1 This painless white lesion was present in a 45-year-old asymptomatic man (non-smoker), who was not known to be at risk of HIV infection. It could not be removed by scraping with a spatula.
(a) What is it?
(b) What is the pathogenesis?
(c) Does it have any clinical significance?

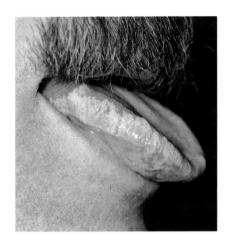

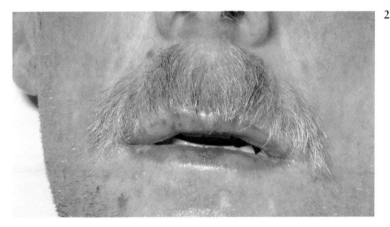

2 This patient was undergoing treatment for cerebral toxoplasmosis when these mucocutaneous lesions and a skin rash developed.
(a) What is the diagnosis?
(b) What is the most likely cause?
(c) What differential diagnoses should be considered?

3

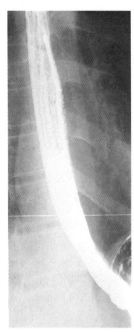

3 This 22-year-old previously asymptomatic night-watchman presented with burning dysphagia, partly relieved by antacids. A barium swallow was performed and is shown here.
(a) What does this show?
(b) What is the most likely diagnosis?
(c) What is the significance of the development of this condition in an HIV-positive individual?

4 This lesion was noted by a dentist when examining an HIV-positive Zambian man.
(a) What is it?
(b) What are the differential diagnoses?
(c) What other signs in the mouth may suggest the presence of HIV infection?

4

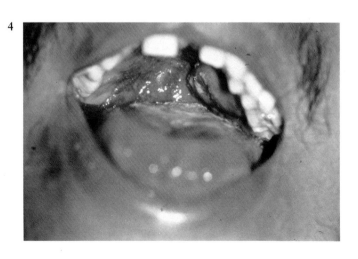

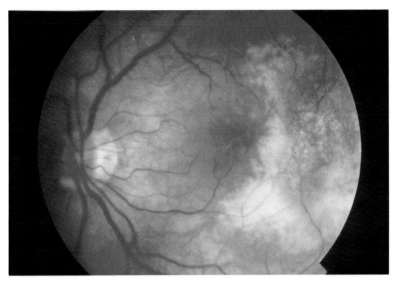

5 This patient complained of visual disturbance, developing over the course of two days.
(a) What condition is this?
(b) What visual field loss did he have?
(c) Is the other eye likely to be affected?

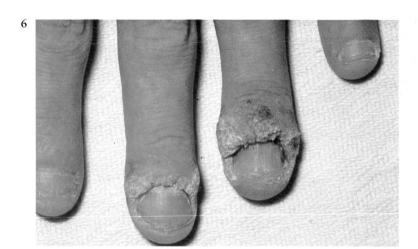

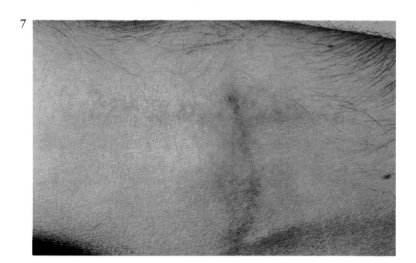

6, 7 An 18-year-old intravenous drug user presented with these peri-ungual lesions. Similar lesions are seen along the lines of the veins.
(a) What is the cause of these lesions?
(b) What phenomenon is shown in 7?
(c) Should this condition make one suspect HIV infection?

8

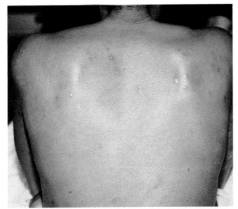

8 An HIV-infected Zambian woman gave a three month history of this intensely itchy maculopapular rash.
(a) What are the differential diagnoses?
(b) What is the approximate male-to-female ratio of HIV infection in central African countries?

9

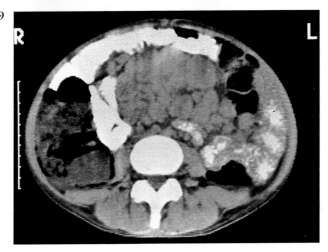

9 A patient with HIV infection, but previously well, presented with weight loss, fevers, persistent diarrhoea and abdominal pain increasing over the last three months, and an abdominal mass. A computerised tomography scan was performed.
(a) What does the scan show?
(b) What are the major differential diagnoses?
(c) What investigation should be performed to confirm the diagnosis?

15

10

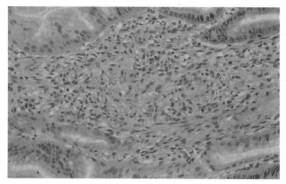

10 An HIV-positive man in his thirties presented with epigastric discomfort, and felt full after eating even small meals ('small stomach syndrome'). Gastric biopsy was performed during an endoscopic examination.
(a) What is the diagnosis?
(b) What practical point should be considered by the endoscopist during attempts to obtain biopsy material for diagnosis of this particular condition?
(c) Where else would one expect to find evidence of this condition in this man?

11

11 A 22-year-old HIV-positive man attended his general practitioner with this rash, which was confined to the trunk, his palms and the soles of his feet being clear. The patient wondered if it was related to his HIV infection.
(a) What is it?
(b) How should the doctor have replied to his question?

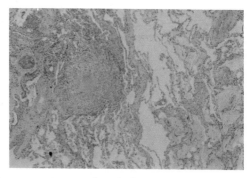

12 A 34-year-old Ugandan man presented with fevers and dyspnoea, and underwent a bronchoscopy and trans-bronchial lung biopsy. He was later found to be infected with HIV. The haematoxylin and eosin stained lung biopsy is shown.
(a) What is the diagnosis?
(b) What would be your initial treatment?
(c) What would be your long-term therapy?

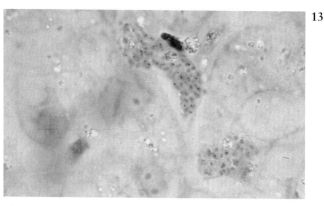

13 A 34-year-old HIV-positive man, originally from Peru, presented with fevers, hepatomegaly, raised serum aspartate aminotransferase, and pancytopenia. He had travelled in the past three years to Greece, Italy and the south of France. A liver biopsy was performed.
(a) Give the diagnosis.
(b) How might the clinical and diagnostic features of this disease in the immunosuppressed differ from those in the immunocompetent?
(c) What is the treatment?

14

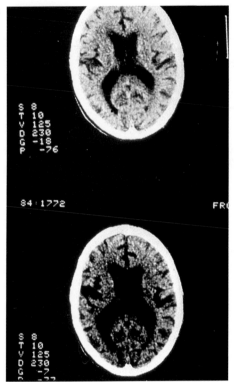

14 This 21-year-old man with AIDS-related complex (CDC group IV C2) presented with loss of short-term memory, change in behaviour, and intellectual deterioration. The main abnormality on examination of the central nervous system (CNS) was truncal ataxia. There were no systemic symptoms. A CT brain scan was performed and is shown below the same cut taken nine months previously.

(a) What abnormalities are shown, and what has happened in the intervening nine months?

(b) What is the most likely diagnosis and what are the differential diagnoses?

(c) What treatment should be offered?

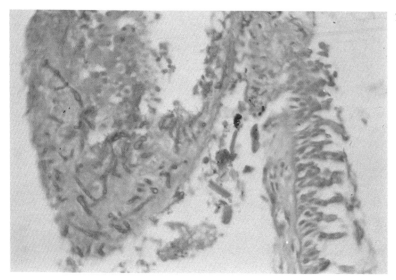

15 An HIV-positive man presented with a three week history of epigastric pain following meals. Oesophagogastroscopy showed inflamed mucosa in the oesophagus associated with white plaques. An oesophageal biopsy was performed.
(a) What is the diagnosis?
(b) What is unusual about this man's history?
(c) How may this condition be diagnosed?

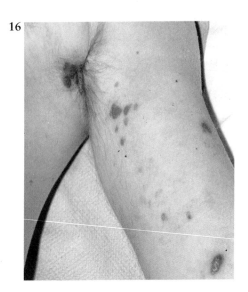

16 These painless, non-itchy, non-ulcerated cutaneous lesions developed over the course of four months in an otherwise fit homosexual man. The lesions stopped increasing in size, and one had recently resolved completely. However, the arm had become swollen over the past two weeks.
(a) What are the lesions?
(b) What would be seen on histology?
(c) What has caused the oedema?

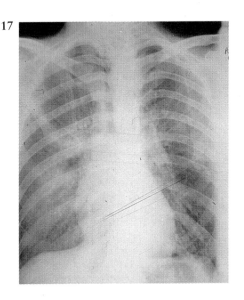

17 This man had just completed a three week course of co-trimoxazole for *Pneumocystis carinii* pneumonia (PCP), diagnosed on an induced sputum sample. The blood gases, after showing initial improvement, deteriorated with the PO_2 falling from 86 to 60mmHg. A repeat chest radiograph also showed deterioration with the appearances shown. Cultures from the initial sputum culture were negative for viruses and bacteria.
(a) What are the three most likely infectious causes for this deterioration?
(b) What is the investigation that should be performed?
(c) Should steroids be given?

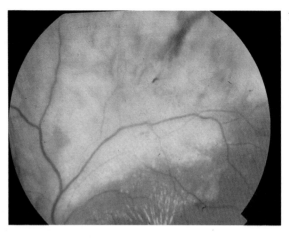

18 This patient was diagnosed with AIDS one year before he presented in clinic with a week's history of 'floaters' in one eye. The eye was not painful and he had no systemic symptoms or signs.
(a) What abnormalities are seen on funduscopy?
(b) What is the most likely diagnosis?
(c) What is the differential diagnosis?

19 This 20-year-old English man developed colicky abdominal pain, diarrhoea, fever and weight loss.
(a) What abnormalities are shown on the abdominal CT scan?
(b) What are the likely differential diagnoses?

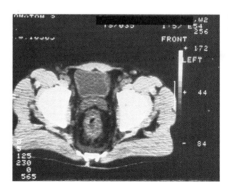

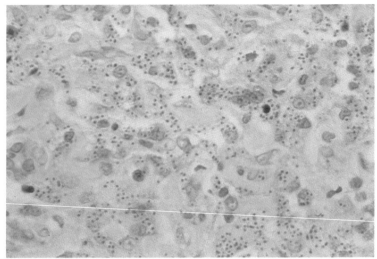

20 This man presented with raised erythematous skin lesions. A skin biopsy was performed and a Giemsa-stained section is shown.
(a) What does the biopsy show?
(b) In what areas of the world is this disease endemic?
(c) How else might this disease present?

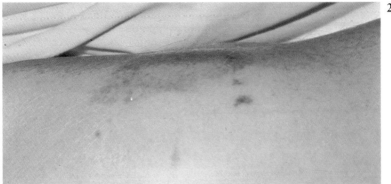

21 An HIV-positive patient presented with a two day history of diarrhoea, fevers and confusion. He attributed the diarrhoea to a meal of cold chicken salad. The only additional findings on examination were mild abdominal tenderness and multiple skin lesions as shown. Gram-negative rods were isolated from blood cultures.
(a) What is the organism most likely to be?
(b) What is the cause of the skin lesions?
(c) How should this case be managed?

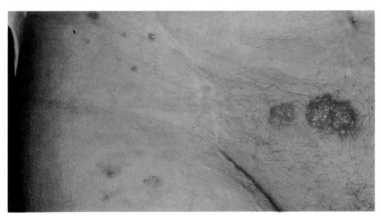

22 This homosexual man, HIV status unknown, presented with pruritus ani, tenesmus and this skin lesion on his abdomen.
(a) What is the most likely diagnosis?
(b) Is this condition HIV-related?

23

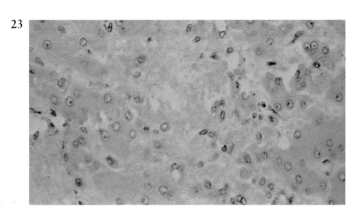

24

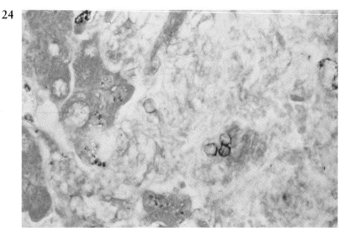

23, 24 Following an episode of *Pneumocystis carinii* pneumonia, this man commenced secondary prophylaxis with nebulised pentamidine. Three months later he developed a pyrexial illness with hepatic failure from which he rapidly died. There were no stigmata of chronic liver disease. The histology of a post-mortem liver biopsy is shown in **23** stained with haematoxylin and eosin (H&E), and in **24** with the Grocott modification of methanamine silver–PAS stain.

(a) What conditions should have been suspected when the patient presented?

(b) What is the diagnosis?

(c) Which other sites may have been affected?

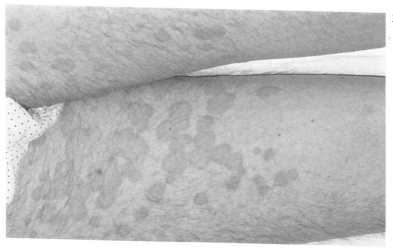

25 This HIV-positive patient presented with an intensely pruritic skin rash. He had recently been discharged from hospital following a diagnosis of *Mycobacterium avium intracellulare* infection (MAI) for which treatment had been started with rifabutin (ansamycin), pyrazinamide, isoniazid and ethambutol. A drug reaction was suspected.
(a) What drug was most likely to have caused this rash?
(b) Which drugs are more frequently associated with hypersensitivity reactions in people with HIV infection?

26 This contrast-enhanced CT brain scan shows a large ring-lesion with surrounding oedema. Other cuts demonstrated further similar abnormalities in this HIV-infected patient with fever and headache. Serology was positive for toxoplasma antibody at low titre, with the comment 'evidence of past infection' from the microbiology reference laboratory.
(a) What is the likely diagnosis?
(b) What features are typical of this?
(c) What is the treatment?

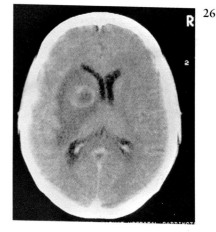

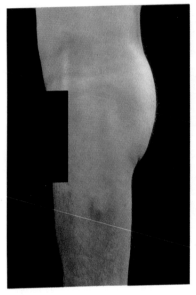 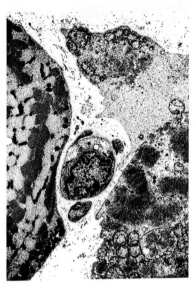

27, 28 A previously healthy 35-year-old man with AIDS presented with a two month history of pains in his thighs and difficulty in walking up stairs. He had been on zidovudine (AZT), 1000mg/day, for 14 months. An open muscle biopsy was taken from the vastus lateralis, and the electron microscopic appearances are shown.

(a) What is the likely diagnosis?

(b) What is the differential diagnosis?

(c) What abnormalities are seen on the muscle biopsy and what investigations might prove helpful?

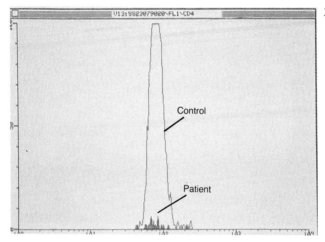

29 This is a flow cytometer analysis of peripheral blood, in which CD4 positive 'helper' T-lymphocytes have been stained with a fluorescent monoclonal antibody. The *x*-axis represents the intensity of fluorescence for the cell population and the *y*-axis the number of CD4 positive cells in an adult patient and healthy control.

(a) What is the abnormality?

(b) What are the causes of this finding?

(c) What factors affect CD4 and CD8 ('suppressor') lymphocyte counts in healthy individuals?

30

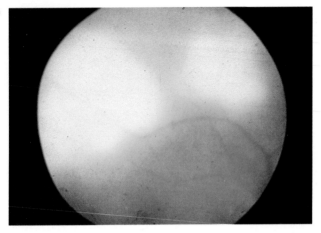

30 A 46-year-old AIDS patient presented to casualty with a fever, painful left eye and visual loss. These large white lesions could be seen protruding into the vitreous.
(a) What are the two most likely diagnoses from the appearance of the retinal lesion?
(b) Are both these conditions typical of HIV-related immune deficiency?
(c) What else should be done?

31

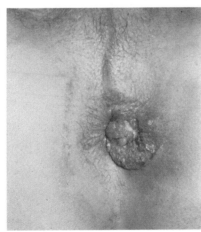

31 This single painless lesion developed over the course of three months in a 38-year-old homosexual man.
(a) What is the likely diagnosis?
(b) Give two differential diagnoses.
(c) Is this lesion HIV-related?

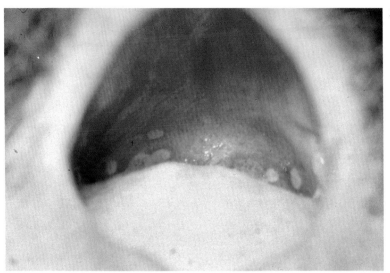

32 These painful pharyngeal ulcers developed over the course of two days. Herpes simplex type 1 was cultured and treatment with intravenous acyclovir commenced as the patient had difficulty in swallowing.

(a) What is the mechanism of action of acyclovir?

(b) After five days of therapy there was no improvement. Give three reasons for this.

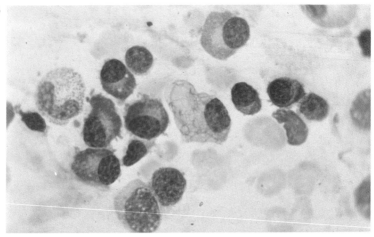

33 A May–Grünwald–Giemsa stain of a bone marrow aspirate from an asymptomatic HIV-positive individual is shown.
(a) What is the abnormality?
(b) What are the causes of this finding?
(c) What serological abnormality, common in HIV infection, may be related to this abnormality?

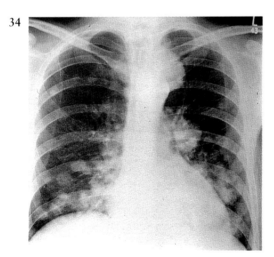

34 This 35-year-old man with AIDS presented with malaise and fever and was found to be neutropenic (0.4 × 10^9/l).
(a) What is the differential diagnosis?
(b) How would you make the diagnosis?
(c) What are the commonest causes of neutropenia in AIDS patients?

35 This patient with AIDS noticed the following appearance on his tongue.
(a) What is the diagnosis?
(b) What is the significance of this condition?
(c) How would you manage this patient?

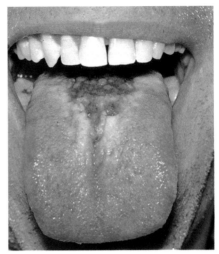

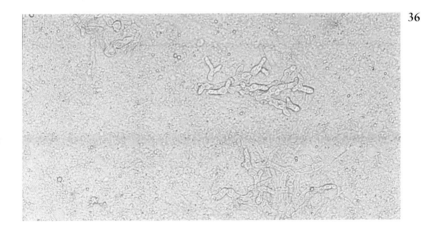

36 This is a medium-power view of unstained material from a liver abscess of a man with AIDS.
(a) What infective organism is seen?
(b) What factors predispose to invasive disease with this organism in:
(i) People with AIDS?
(ii) Those without HIV infection?

37 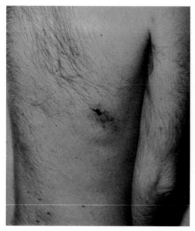  38

37, 38 This HIV-positive patient presented with these painless skin lesions (a biopsy scar is also seen). Six months previously he had varicella zoster infection at this site, involving the eighth to tenth thoracic dermatomes.

(a) What is the clinical significance of the history of multi-dermatomal shingles?

(b) What are the major differential diagnoses of these lesions?

(c) What other skin lesion is demonstrated?

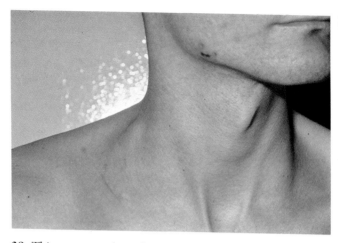

39 This man, seen by a doctor in the accident and emergency department, had a one month history of night sweats and mild lethargy.

(a) Initially, before a history of HIV is obtained, what diagnoses should be considered?

Subsequently, a history was obtained of a recent episode of *Pneumocystis carinii* pneumonia (PCP), which was the patient's first AIDS diagnosis.

(b) What are the most likely differential diagnoses now?

(c) What diagnostic procedure should be performed?

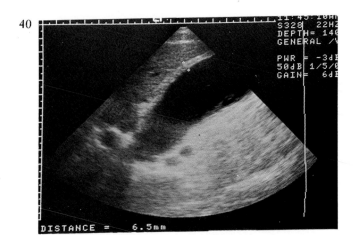

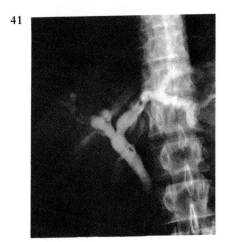

40, 41 This AIDS patient presented with fever, right-sided abdominal pain, and raised serum alkaline phosphatase, transaminases and bilirubin.

(a) What abnormalities are seen on the abdominal ultrasound in **40** and what are the likely causes?

(b) What abnormalities are shown on the endoscopic retrograde cholangiopancreatogram (ERCP) in **41** and what are the causes?

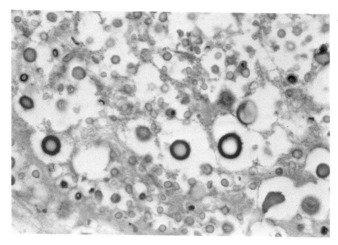

42 An HIV-positive man presented with a rash which was acneiform in appearance, but did not respond to conventional therapy for this condition. A skin biopsy was performed and a mucicarmine stained section is shown.
(a) What is the diagnosis?
(b) What are the usual presentations of this disease?
(c) Name other conditions associated with HIV infection where internal disease may first manifest itself in the skin.

43

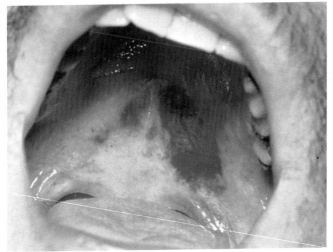

43 This patient with extensive gastro-intestinal Kaposi's sarcoma (KS), including this lesion on the palate, had undergone systemic chemotherapy with vinblastine eight days previously.
(a) What complication of the chemotherapy has occurred?
(b) What other causes should be considered for this appearance?
(c) He is also on the anti-HIV agent zidovudine (AZT). Should the drug be stopped?

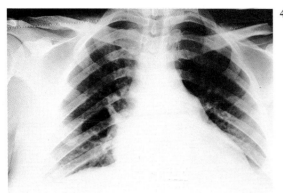

44, 45 A 28-year-old African woman, known to be HIV-positive, presented with headache for one week, and a mild cough and low-grade pyrexia (37.4°C). There were no meningeal signs or focal neurology, and CT scan of the brain was normal. The first chest X-ray (**44**) is before treatment, and the second (**45**) is after one week's therapy. Lumbar puncture revealed the diagnosis.

(a) What is the likely diagnosis?
(b) How might the disease present?
(c) What is the therapy?

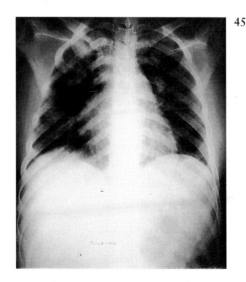

46

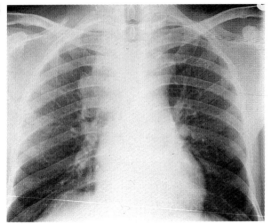

46 This HIV-positive man presented with night sweats and had lost 6 kg in weight over four months.
(a) What does the chest radiograph show?
(b) What are the main differential diagnoses?
(c) What further investigations would you consider?

47

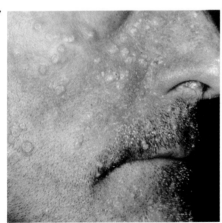

47 These pearly, umbilicated lesions are restricted to the face of this patient.
(a) What are they?
(b) What is the cause?
(c) Why should immune deficiency be suspected in this patient?

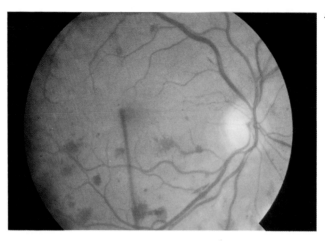

48 This 52-year-old HIV-positive insulin-dependent diabetic was noted to have these retinal changes on routine funduscopy.
(a) What abnormalities are shown?
(b) What is the most likely diagnosis?
(c) Will his diabetic control be affected by the HIV infection?

49 This is a transbronchial biopsy from a patient with suspected *Pneumocystis carinii* pneumonia (PCP). The specimen has stained positive with immunoperoxidase monoclonal antibodies to *Pneumocystis*.
(a) What is the value of monoclonal staining for *Pneumocystis*?
(b) What tests, other than bronchoscopy, may suggest or diagnose PCP?
(c) What advantage does bronchoscopy have over empirical treatment in a suspected case of PCP?

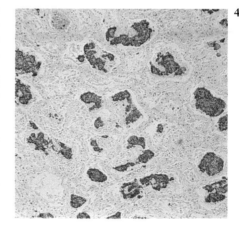

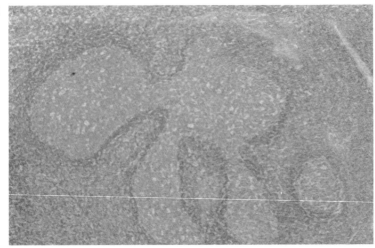

50, 51 These two lymph node biopsies were taken from the same HIV-positive man at an interval of ten months.
(a) What condition is represented by both pictures?
(b) Describe the histological features shown.
(c) What is the prognostic significance of the features seen in **51**?

52 This patient had just been diagnosed with cytomegalovirus retinitis and required maintenance therapy with intravenous ganciclovir several times each week.

(a) What surgical procedure has been performed?

(b) What are the advantages of this technique?

(c) What is the most serious potential long-term complication of this procedure?

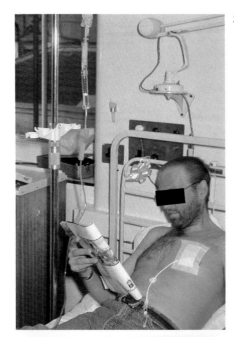

53 This 32-year-old man underwent a successful cardiac transplant and continued on cyclosporin A immunosuppression to prevent rejection. He presented with a one week history of increasing confusion, headache and fevers.

(a) What does the CT scan demonstrate?

(b) What would be the most likely causes of these lesions in this individual?

(c) What investigations should be performed?

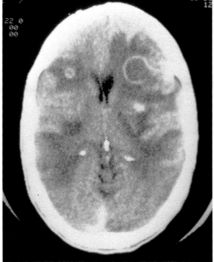

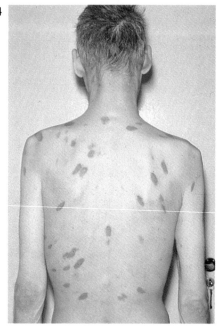

54 This intravenous drug user had had an 18 month history of cutaneous Kaposi's sarcoma (KS) when he presented with a rapid acceleration in the size and number of lesions.

(a) What characteristic pattern of distribution of KS lesions is shown?

(b) Why should risk factors for HIV infection other than IV drug abuse be suspected in this individual?

(c) Why might the KS have become so active recently?

55 A sexually active homosexual man with persistent pruritus ani had a perianal biopsy.

(a) What abnormalities are seen?

(b) Which viral infection is associated with these changes?

(c) What condition is associated with infection by this virus?

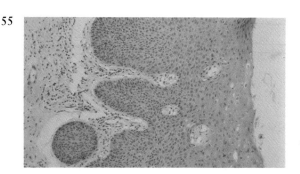

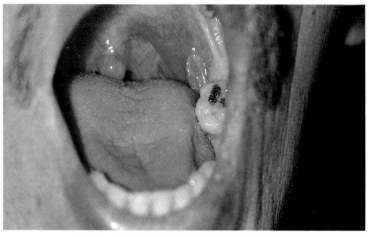

56 This patient with AIDS developed painful bilateral pharyngeal ulcers over the course of seven days.
(a) What diagnoses should be considered?
(b) How could the diagnosis be confirmed?
(c) What symptomatic treatments are useful?

57 This is a chest radiograph of an HIV-positive man who presented with respiratory failure.
(a) What is the most likely diagnosis?
(b) What is the main differential diagnosis?
(c) What factors may have altered the severity of *Pneumocystis carinii* pneumonia (PCP) in our patients over the past four years?

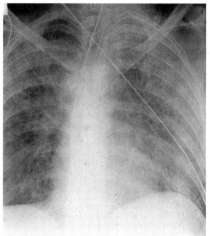

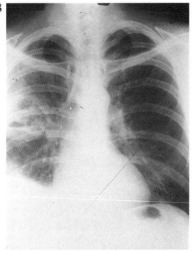

58 An HIV-positive man, who was a heavy smoker, presented with a seven week history of cough and fevers.
(a) What is the likely cause of this abnormal chest radiograph?
(b) What is the differential diagnosis?

59

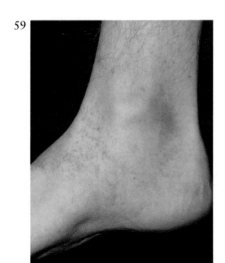

59 This previously well young man presented with spontaneous bruising of the skin during the past two months and bleeding of the gums on brushing his teeth. He had no other physical signs. His platelet count was 5×10^9, but the rest of his blood count was normal.
(a) Name two possible diagnoses.
(b) What questions should he be asked?
(c) How would you investigate and treat him?

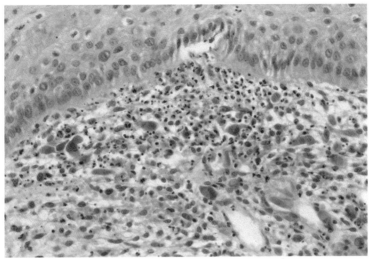

60 A person with AIDS presented with dysphagia which did not respond to empirical therapy with ketoconazole or acyclovir. Endoscopy revealed a shallow ulcer in the lower oesophagus which was biopsied.
(a) What does the biopsy show?
(b) What other sites may be involved in people with AIDS?
(c) What is the therapy?

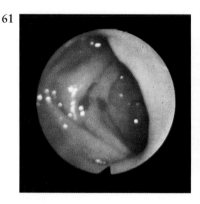 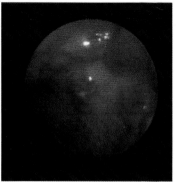

61, 62 This patient, known to have AIDS, presented with nausea and epigastric discomfort. An endoscopy was performed and the appearance of the stomach is illustrated (**61**). Also shown is the endoscopic view of the stomach five months later (**62**).
(a) What is the diagnosis?
(b) What would endoscopic biopsy at both stages show?
(c) How would you treat this condition?

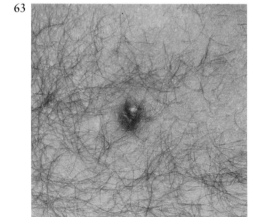

63 A male patient was referred to the surgical outpatient department for excision biopsy of this exquisitely tender purple nodule on his knee.
(a) What is the most likely diagnosis?
(b) What are the typical histological features of this lesion?
(c) What feature suggests that this is not Kaposi's sarcoma (KS)?

64 A 34-year-old homosexual man presented with this extensive itchy maculo-papular rash, which developed four days after starting penicillin for a sore throat. An HIV antibody test was negative one month previously.

(a) Give three possible causes of the rash.

(b) What investigations would you perform?

(c) What change in treatment should be made while awaiting the results?

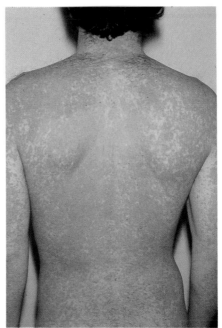

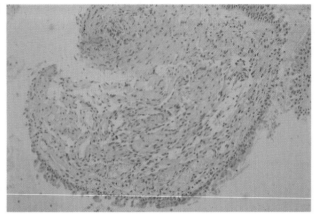

65 A 29-year-old non-smoker with AIDS, whose only previous disease was *Pneumocystis carinii* pneumonia, presented with dyspnoea. Chest X-ray showed left lower lobe collapse. Bronchoscopy showed a reddish lesion obstructing the left lower main bronchus. The lesion was biopsied.

(a) What is the diagnosis?
(b) How is this diagnosis usually made?
(c) What are the main complications of this condition?

66 This AIDS patient presented with severe dysphagia. The oropharynx is shown.

(a) What is the most likely cause of the dysphagia?
(b) What is the treatment?
(c) What other causes for the dysphagia should be considered?

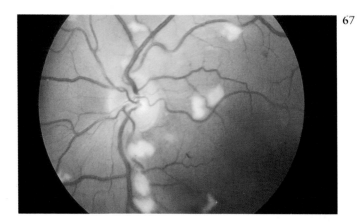

67 These asymptomatic lesions were seen on funduscopy of an asymptomatic HIV-positive patient.
(a) What are the lesions?
(b) What is the pathogenesis?
(c) What treatment is required?

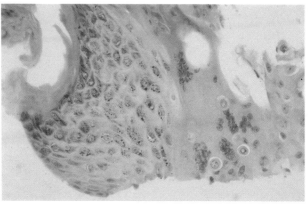

68 An HIV-positive female had painful vulval and perianal ulcers which were biopsied.
(a) What abnormalities are seen?
(b) What is the likely diagnosis?
(c) Name other causes of perianal ulceration which may be associated with HIV infection.

69

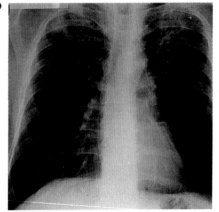

70

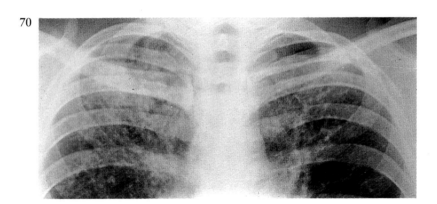

69, 70 This man, known to be HIV-positive, had a non-productive cough and mild dyspnoea for two weeks, and a low-grade pyrexia (37.6°C). A chest X-ray (**69**) is shown accompanied by a close-up view of the apices (**70**).
(a) What is the most likely diagnosis?
(b) Name another possible diagnosis.
(c) How would you investigate this patient?

71 A young man, with previously asymptomatic HIV infection, presented with a five week history of mild dysphagia. No abnormalities were found on physical examination. A barium swallow was performed.
(a) What is your differential diagnosis?
(b) How would you attempt to make a definitive diagnosis?
(c) What are the therapeutic options?

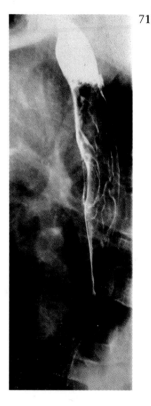

72 A previously asymptomatic HIV-positive man developed unilateral non-tender cervical lymphadenopathy of the anterior triangle, weight loss, fevers and drenching night sweats. No other lymph nodes or masses were palpable and the clinical examination is otherwise normal. He had no travel history of note. A needle biopsy revealed necrotic tissue only.
(a) What two diagnoses are most likely in this patient?
(b) What features point to these diagnoses?
(c) How would you confirm the diagnosis?

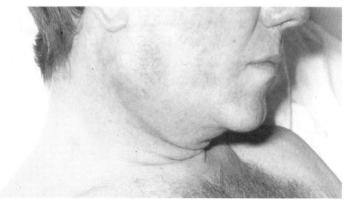

73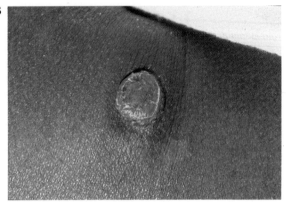

73 This lesion on the leg was first noted by this Ugandan man four months previously. On examination he had extensive oral candidiasis and complained of burning dysphagia.

(a) What is the most likely diagnosis of the skin lesion?

(b) What groups of individuals are particularly at risk for this condition?

74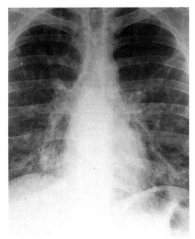

74 An AIDS patient, previously diagnosed with *Pneumocystis carinii* pneumonia, cutaneous Kaposi's sarcoma (KS) and oesophageal candidiasis, presented with a five week history of increasing shortness of breath.

(a) What is the most likely diagnosis?

(b) How would you confirm the diagnosis?

75 This skin condition is frequently associated with HIV infection.
(a) What are the lesions?
(b) What are the major differential diagnoses?
(c) How could the diagnosis be confirmed?

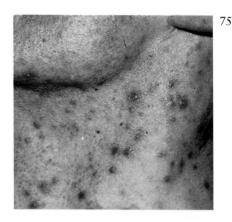

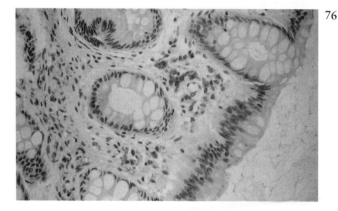

76 This patient was first diagnosed with AIDS two years previously, and had suffered two episodes of *Pneumocystis carinii* pneumonia and cerebral toxoplasmosis since then. He presented with pancytopenia, fever, weight loss and diarrhoea. A rectal biopsy was performed and acid-fast bacilli demonstrated as shown.
(a) What is unusual about the histological appearances of this mycobacterial infection in comparison to one in the immunocompetent host?
(b) What type of mycobacteria would be most likely to be cultured from the biopsy in this particular patient?
(c) What is the most likely cause of the pancytopenia?

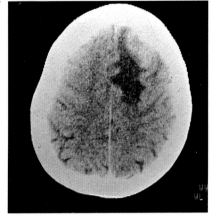

77 This patient with known HIV infection dating back six years was brought to casualty in status epilepticus and found to have a low-grade fever. Friends said that he had been completely well and at work until four days previously. A contrast enhanced CT scan was performed and showed a solitary lesion.

(a) What is the differential diagnosis of this lesion?

(b) What diagnostic procedure should be considered?

(c) What specific treatment should be given in addition to controlling his fits until diagnosis is confirmed?

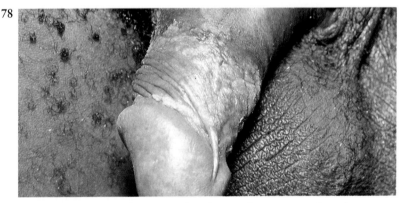

78 This patient with AIDS-related complex presented with pruritic lesions on his penis and perineum. His girlfriend had similar perianal lesions and they both asked if they had herpes simplex infection.

(a) What is the diagnosis?

(b) What treatment is available?

(c) What serious complication could result from this condition in both the man and his girlfriend?

79 A 38-year-old man from west Africa presented with fever, confusion, widespread crusted skin ulcers and dysphagia. He was found to be HIV-antibody-positive. The endoscopic appearances of the lower part of his oesophagus are shown. Despite treatment he died ten days after admission.
(a) What is the likely cause of the findings in his oesophagus?
(b) How might his confusion and skin ulcers be explained?
(c) How would you manage a case such as this?

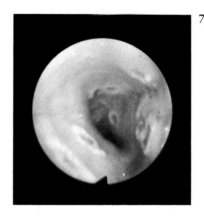

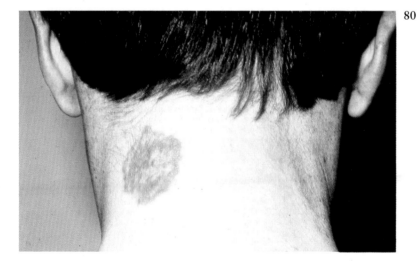

80 This itchy though painless lesion, on the neck of a patient who had had asymptomatic HIV infection for four years, had been increasing in size gradually over the three months preceding presentation. There were no other similar lesions.
(a) What is the lesion?
(b) What is the differential diagnosis?
(c) Is it clinically significant in this patient?

81 A 56-year-old man with AIDS developed worsening dysphagia over a five week period. A barium swallow was performed.
(a) On the history alone, what is the most likely diagnosis?
(b) What is the most likely explanation of the radiological appearances in this case?
(c) What other cause, unrelated to HIV infection, could explain the main radiological abnormality?

82 This known HIV-positive patient presented with swelling of the face, which was pronounced in the periorbital region as shown.
(a) What non-HIV-related diagnoses should be considered as a cause for the periorbital swelling?
(b) It was felt that an HIV-related diagnosis was most likely. What was this diagnosis?
(c) How would you manage the patient?

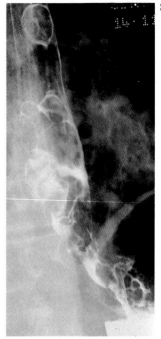

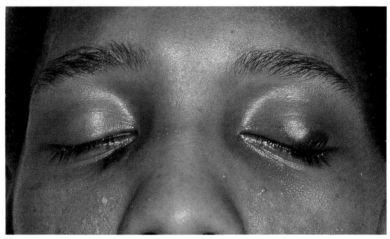

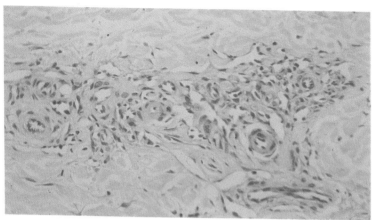

83 A 35-year-old male, with no medical history, presented to a dermatologist with a small (5 mm) crimson lesion on the skin of his thigh. The lesion was biopsied.
(a) Describe the histological abnormalities.
(b) What is the diagnosis?
(c) What sites other than the skin are commonly affected by this condition?

84 A homosexual man with a history of *Pneumocystis carinii* pneumonia (PCP) six months previously presented with this painful perianal lesion. He had not had lesions like this in the past.
(a) What is the most likely diagnosis?
(b) How would you confirm this?
(c) What is the differential diagnosis?

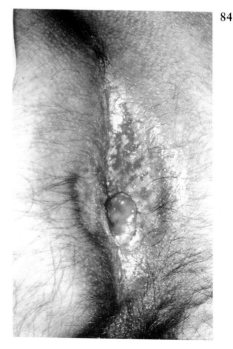

85

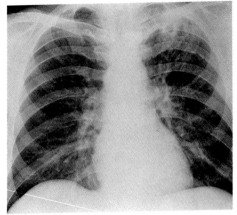

85 A 40-year-old HIV-positive intravenous drug user with AIDS presented with weight loss, malaise and low-grade pyrexias. A Mantoux test was negative. His chest X ray is shown.
(a) What is the most likely diagnosis?
(b) Suggest another diagnosis.
(c) How would you investigate this man?

86

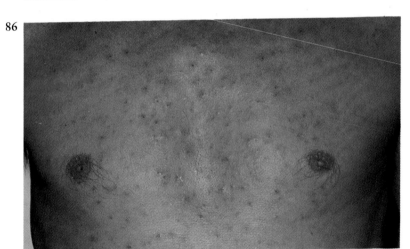

86 Folliculitis is seen more frequently in individuals with HIV infection than in the general population. This patient had recurrent folliculitis due to *Staphylococcus aureus*, but was otherwise asymptomatic.
(a) What general measures should be taken to reduce the risk of recurrence?
(b) Which aspect of the immune system is thought to be important in the control of such infections?
(c) Why should this be defective in a patient with HIV infection?

87 This cachetic Zambian man has HIV-related 'Slim disease', which is characterised by a diarrhoeal illness, with marked weight loss and fever.
(a) In which African countries does HIV-1 occur?
(b) Where is HIV-2 most frequently found?
(c) Which infectious complications of HIV-related immune deficiency would be most likely to occur in this man?

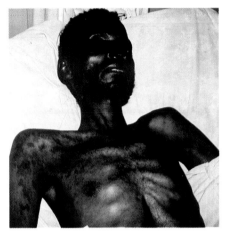

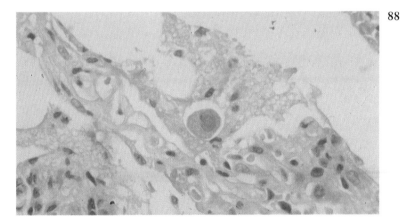

88 A man known to have AIDS presented with cough, slight dyspnoea, and patchy bilateral shadowing on chest X-ray. He had a bronchoscopy during which a trans-bronchial biopsy was performed. The specimen was treated with the haematoxylin and eosin stain.
(a) There is evidence of two infective organisms on the biopsy. Name them.
(b) What is the significance of these two organisms to the man's pulmonary disease?
(c) How would you manage this case?

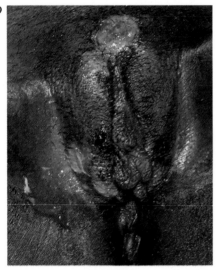

89 This woman from central Africa was known to be HIV-antibody-positive.
(a) What is the likely diagnosis?
(b) What other infectious diseases may give a similar appearance?
(c) How would you manage this woman?

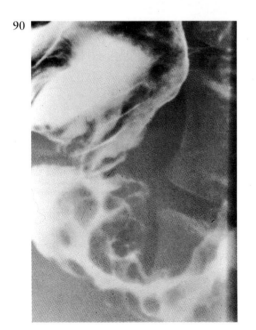

90 A man with AIDS and cutaneous Kaposi's sarcoma presented with epigastric pain. He had just completed a six week course of systemic corticosteroids for a severe exacerbation of his bronchial asthma. The patient thought that the steroids had brought on his symptoms. The doctor seeing him thought that he probably had peptic ulceration secondary to the steroids and arranged a barium meal.
(a) Was the doctor correct in his diagnosis?
(b) Could the patient be correct in his assumption?
(c) What are the dangers of steroid use in people with HIV infection?

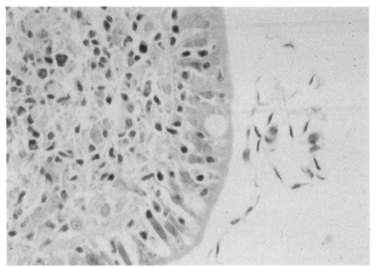

91 A 42-year-old HIV-positive man presented with intermittent diarrhoea and abdominal discomfort of 60 days' duration. Rectal biopsy and three stool examinations were negative, but the duodenal biopsy is shown.
(a) What is the diagnosis and treatment?
(b) What other diagnostic tests are useful for this condition?
(c) What other bowel infections are associated with HIV infection?

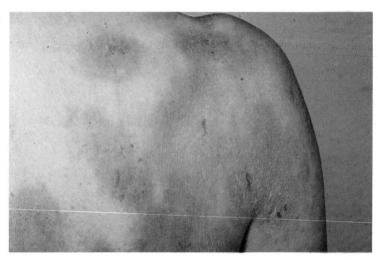

92 This patient presented with the skin lesions shown. Both an HIV-related and non-HIV-related diagnosis were considered.
(a) What is the most likely HIV-related diagnosis?
(b) What is the most likely non-HIV-related diagnosis?
(c) What investigation would give the diagnosis?

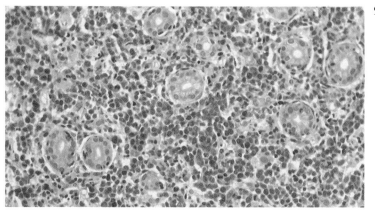

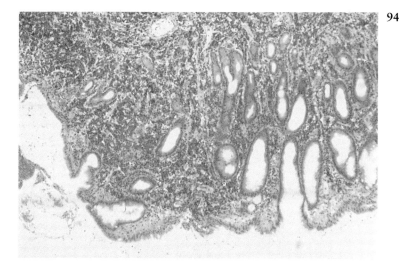

93, 94 A man known to have AIDS had a ten week history of weight loss and night sweats, and a one month history of fullness after eating small meals. A gastroscopy was performed and the gastric mucosa biopsied. (High-power view top, lower-power above.)

(a) What is the diagnosis?

(b) What histological types of this condition are seen in AIDS?

(c) What sites does this condition particularly affect in AIDS?

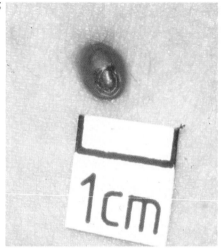

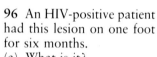

95 This 35-year-old man had several of these lesions on his lower limbs. He was known to be HIV-positive and there was no history of local injury.
(a) What is the differential diagnosis?
(b) Histology of a lesion demonstrated slit-like spaces formed by proliferating spindle-shaped cells which contained red blood cells. What is the lesion?
(c) Are these lesions radio-sensitive?

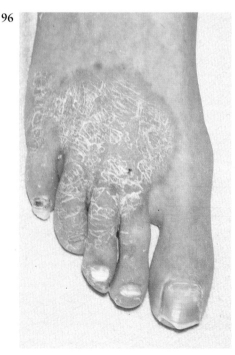

96 An HIV-positive patient had this lesion on one foot for six months.
(a) What is it?
(b) What is the treatment?
(c) What is the significance?

97 This is the chest radiograph of an HIV-positive man who presented with cough, dyspnoea and malaise.
(a) Describe the radiological appearances.
(b) What is the most likely diagnosis?
(c) Suggest possible alternative diagnoses.

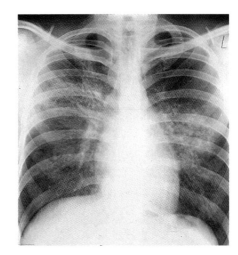

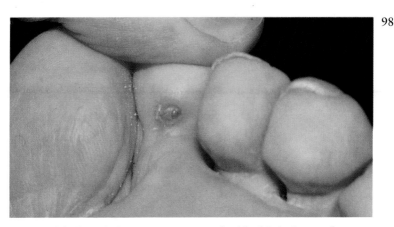

98 An elderly Polish woman presented with this lesion on her toe.
(a) What is this lesion? Give a differential diagnosis.
(b) In what groups of HIV-negative patients is this condition found?
(c) In what groups of HIV-positive patients is this lesion common?

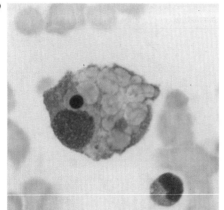

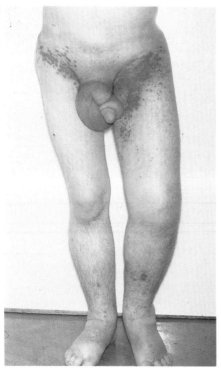

99 A 22-year-old Ugandan man presented to casualty with a two week history of fevers, weight loss and shortness of breath. On examination he was febrile at 40°C, with generalised lymphadenopathy and hepatosplenomegaly. A bone marrow aspirate was performed (May – Grünwald – Giemsa stain).
(a) What abnormality is shown?
(b) What are the causes of this?
(c) What peripheral blood findings are associated with this marrow picture?

100 This AIDS patient had extensive cutaneous Kaposi's sarcoma (KS), with bilateral inguinal lymph node involvement. He then presented with acute onset of pain and swelling of the left leg.
(a) What three main causes for the presentation should be considered?
(b) What investigations should be performed?
(c) What features of the pathogenesis of KS explain the lymph node involvement?

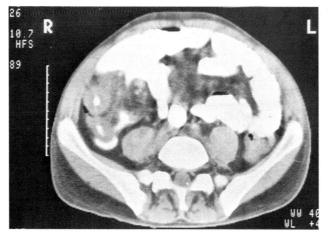

101 A 38-year-old man presented with colicky abdominal pain and weight loss. Although AIDS with oesophageal candidiasis had been diagnosed ten months previously, no other HIV-related condition had been identified – apart from two small cutaneous Kaposi's sarcoma (KS) lesions, which were not active. Initial investigations, including gastroduodenoscopy, were normal and a CT scan of the abdomen was performed.
(a) What is the differential diagnosis?
(b) What other investigations might help in the diagnosis of this man's disease?

102

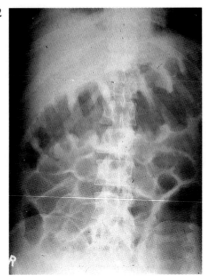

102 This AIDS patient presented to his general practitioner with abdominal pain of four days' duration. Examination revealed a mild generalised abdominal tenderness and distension, although there was considerable rebound tenderness. A plain abdominal X-ray is shown.
(a) What is the most likely diagnosis?
(b) Suggest alternative diagnoses.
(c) What is the investigation of choice?

103

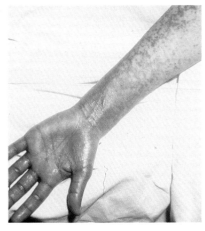

103 The skin lesions shown are due to graft-versus-host disease (GVHD) in a patient 2 months after an otherwise uneventful bone marrow transplant with complete engraftment. The patient is maintained on cyclosporin A and methylprednisolone immunosuppression. She complains of haematuria and bilateral loin pain.
(a) What are the likely opportunist causes of haematuria in this patient?
(b) How could the most likely of these be diagnosed?
(c) From what other infections will she be at risk?

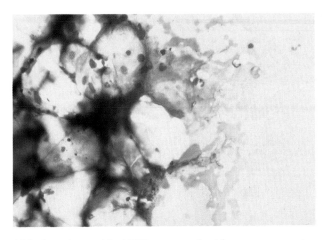

104 A patient with AIDS presented with a gram-negative septicaemia and was found to be pancytopenic. He was on zidovudine (AZT) as anti-HIV therapy, ganciclovir for cytomegalovirus retinitis, ketoconazole as secondary prophylaxis for oral candidiasis and pyrimethamine with sulfadoxine as maintenance therapy for cerebral toxoplasmosis. A bone marrow aspirate is shown (May–Grünwald–Giemsa stain).
(a) What is the abnormality?
(b) Which of the drugs *does not* cause pancytopenia?

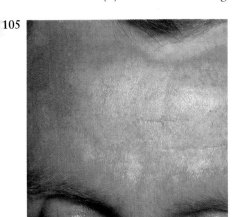

105 This HIV-positive man noticed increased pigmentation on his forehead after a sunny holiday. There were no other similar patches and he was otherwise completely well, with no other abnormalities on clinical examination.
(a) What is the condition and the differential diagnosis?
(b) What are the most common associations of this condition?
(c) Is it HIV-related?

106

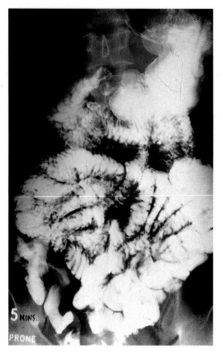

106 A known AIDS patient had a four month history of colicky abdominal pain, diarrhoea and weight loss. Upper gastrointestinal endoscopy was normal, and the patient had a barium meal and follow-through.
(a) What is the differential diagnosis?
(b) What other investigations might indicate the presence of the diseases you have considered?
(c) Name a condition not associated with HIV infection which would give similar clinical features and radiological appearances.

107

107 Patients waiting to attend a mixed general medicine and HIV clinic in Zambia.
(a) What are the most important risk factors for HIV infection in Africa?
(b) What are the main differences in disease presentation between AIDS patients in Africa and those in North America or Europe?
(c) What are the main differences in the type of management required by patients from these two areas of the world?

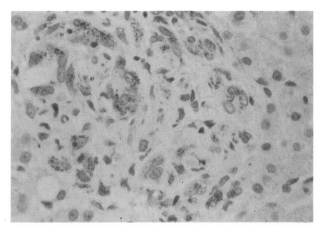

108 A young HIV-positive male gave a five week history of increasing malaise, night sweats and fevers. His liver was enlarged 2 cm below the costal margin, and the serum aspartate transaminase and alkaline phosphatase were slightly raised. A liver biopsy was performed and the Ziehl–Neelsen stain used.
(a) Give two differential diagnoses and suggest which is the most likely.
(b) How might the diagnosis be confirmed?
(c) Suggest the stage of HIV infection and degree of immunosuppression in this man prior to the onset of his present illness.

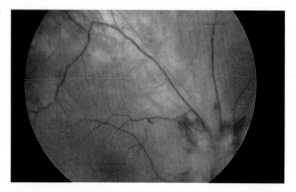

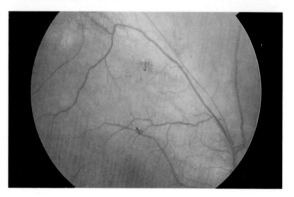

109, 110 These two retinal photographs of the same eye were taken two weeks apart.

(a) What is the infection?

(b) What changes have occurred in the time between the taking of the photographs and what is the likely cause?

(c) What late complication of this condition can lead to blindness, even if the active infection is controlled?

111 A 32-year-old HIV-positive Ugandan woman presented with a six month history of weight loss, persistent diarrhoea and low-grade fevers. Over the past seven days she had deteriorated rapidly with increasing fever, confusion and severe headache. On examination she was dehydrated and unable to give a history. No neck stiffness, photophobia or focal signs were detected. Examination showed the fundi to be normal. A CT brain scan was performed as shown.

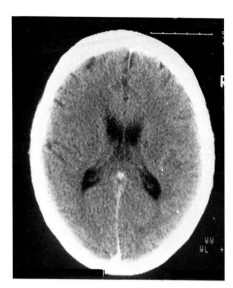

(a) What does the CT scan show?

(b) What are the two most likely diagnoses in this patient?

(c) What investigation should now be performed to confirm the diagnosis?

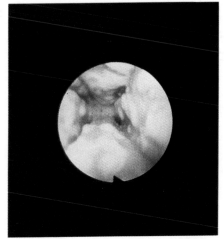

112 A 39-year-old man, known to have AIDS-related complex, presented with intense dysphagia. He had been on ketoconazole for the
past five months as maintenance therapy following successful treatment of oral candidiasis. Two months previously his family practitioner started him on the H-2 blocker cimetidine for suspected acid
reflux. Endoscopy showed this appearance in the oesophagus.
(a) What is the diagnosis?
(b) What is the prognosis?
(c) How would you treat this man?

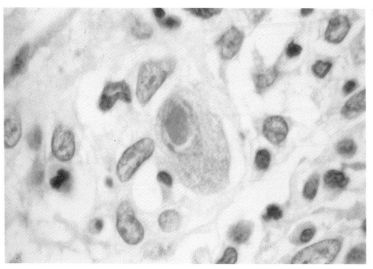

113 A known HIV-positive patient presented with abdominal pain, rebound tenderness, diarrhoea and fevers. Plain X-ray of the abdomen was normal, and stool samples negative on bacterial, mycobacterial and fungal cultures or direct staining for *Cryptosporidium*. A rectal biopsy is shown.
(a) What characteristic pathological feature is shown?
(b) Where else should you look for infection with this organism?
(c) Is the presence of the organism at this site likely to be the cause of the symptoms?

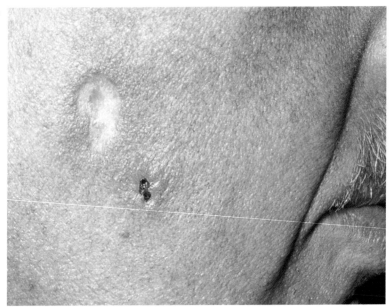

114 An air steward presented with these two painless, ulcerated lesions on his cheek which continued to increase in size during the next two months. He was known to be HIV-antibody-positive. The only other relevant medical history was of seminoma 15 years previously. Repeated bacterial cultures were negative.
(a) What three tumours could be implicated in this situation?
(b) What other infections are possible alternative diagnoses in the light of the negative culture results?
(c) Two biopsies failed to reveal a diagnosis and the patient declined a third. Empirical anti-tuberculous therapy with isoniazid, rifampicin and pyrazinamide was commenced and the lesions shrank. Apart from their anti-TB effect, how might these drugs have effected a response?

115 This HIV-positive man had similar lesions bilaterally in the naso-labial folds, on the forehead and chest.
(a) What is the condition?
(b) Is his HIV status relevant to its presentation?
(c) What is the treatment?

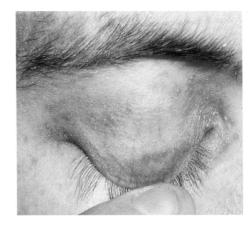

116 This is the barium enema of a man who gave a history of constipation for the past four weeks and more recently developed severe colicky abdominal pain. He also has extensive cutaneous Kaposi's sarcoma (KS).
(a) What is the likely diagnosis?
(b) What conditions not associated with HIV infection could also explain this barium enema appearance?
(c) What are the main complications that might develop in this man due to his bowel disease?

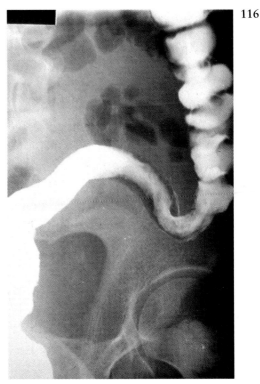

117

117 This Libyan man presented with a six month history of symmetrical peripheral lymphadenopathy and was found to be HIV-positive. He was otherwise completely asymptomatic.
(a) What is the most likely cause of the lymphadenopathy?
(b) What would the histology of a lymph node biopsy show?
(c) What other conditions should be excluded in this particular patient?

118

118 A 52-year-old man with AIDS-related complex presented with headaches and tiredness. On examination he was found to have a left lower quadrantic hemianopia. A contrast enhanced CT scan of the brain is shown.
(a) Name the likely diagnosis with your reasons and suggest another possible diagnosis.
(b) How should this patient be investigated further?
(c) What treatment is available?

119 During the first episode of *Pneumocystis carinii* pneumonia (PCP) a homosexual patient developed pruritic lesions which then became painful and ulcerated.
(a) What are they?
(b) What is the differential diagnosis?
(c) What is the treatment?

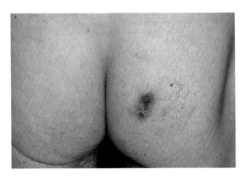

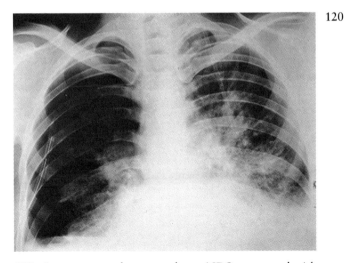

120 A young man, known to have AIDS, presented with sudden onset of dyspnoea.
(a) What is the main abnormality on the chest radiograph?
(b) What is the most likely cause in this patient?
(c) What is the other major cause of this X-ray appearance in AIDS?

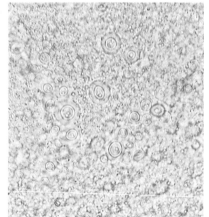

121 A 45-year-old man with longstanding and severe complications of AIDS presented with drowsiness and headache. He had previously clearly stated that he did not wish for any further active management and had repeated this request to his family the day before admission. He died the day after entering hospital and an unstained post-mortem brain biopsy specimen is shown.
(a) What is the diagnosis?
(b) How might the diagnosis be made in life?
(c) How can one decide if treatment has been successful?

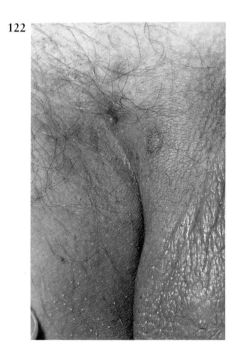

122 This 46-year-old HIV-negative man had been receiving chemotherapy for the treatment of acute myeloid leukaemia and had a neutrophil count of 0.1×10^9/l. Over a matter of four hours he became shocked, with a temperature of 41°C. These lesions were noted in the groin and on the trunk.
(a) What is the name of this condition?
(b) What organism causes these lesions?
(c) What other organisms commonly cause septicaemia in neutropenic patients?

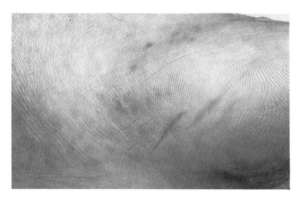

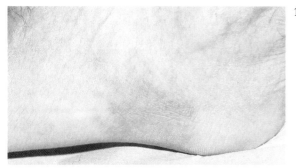

123, 124 A 28-year-old man with known HIV infection noticed these painless, non-pruritic, erythematous lesions on the medial and lateral aspects of the foot. They had developed over the course of two months and more recently were associated with swelling of the foot in the evenings.
(a) What is the most likely diagnosis?
(b) Where else may lesions be found?
(c) Should the lesion be biopsied?

125

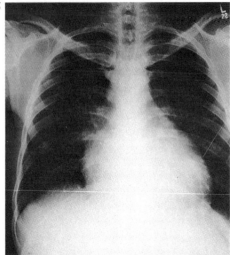

125 A 38-year-old HIV-positive man complained of night sweats and of feeling tired after minimal exertion. His chest radiograph is shown.
(a) What is the differential diagnosis in this man?
(b) What investigation would you ask for next?

126

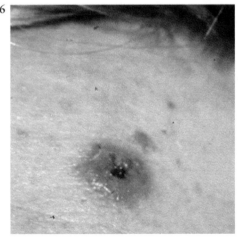

126 This 35-year-old HIV-positive English man had worked in Trinidad and the mid-west USA for ten years. He presented with a one-month history of fevers, increasing cough and shortness of breath. The chest radiograph showed multiple small calcified nodular opacities. Necrotic skin lesions were present as shown, and these were positive with silver stain on skin biopsy histology.
(a) What is the most likely diagnosis?
(b) Is this a recently acquired infection?
(c) What is the treatment?

127, 128 This HIV-infected man presented in casualty with a recent onset of severe abdominal pain. He had had drenching night sweats for the previous six weeks, weight loss and low-grade pyrexias.

(a) What does the plain X-ray of the abdomen show?

(b) What abnormality within the small bowel lumen (arrow) is suggested by the CT scan of the abdomen?

(c) What is the differential diagnosis?

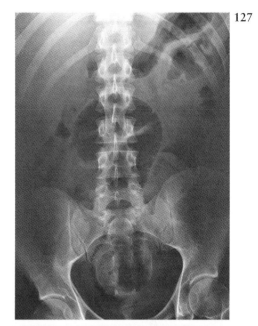

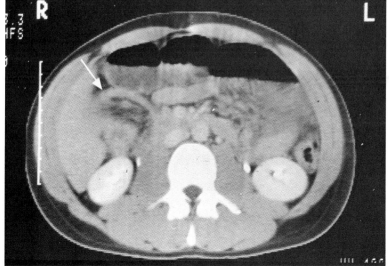

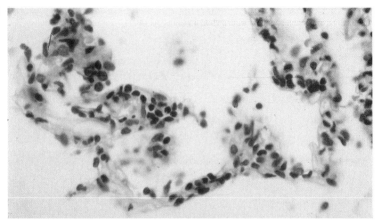

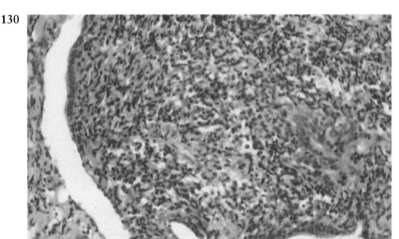

129, 130 A 34-year-old HIV-positive man presented with a two month history of gradually worsening dyspnoea. Chest X-ray showed reticulonodular shadowing, but examination of broncho-alveolar lavage fluid was normal. A transbronchial biopsy was per-formed, two high-power views of which are shown.
(a) What is the diagnosis?
(b) In which group of HIV-positive patients does this disease usually present?
(c) How can this disease present and what treatment is available?

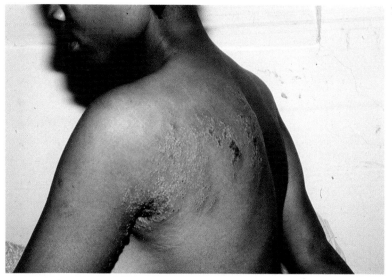

131 This Zambian woman developed a painful ulcerated rash on her trunk as shown.
(a) What is the diagnosis?
(b) Why is this suggestive of underlying immune deficiency?
(c) Is this condition infectious?

132 This solitary lesion appeared on the hand of a previously asymptomatic homosexual man. He was worried by the appearance of the lesion and because it bled very easily.
(a) What is the most likely diagnosis?
(b) What features shown suggest this?
(c) Why is it unlikely to be Kaposi's sarcoma (KS)?

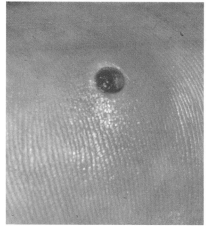

133

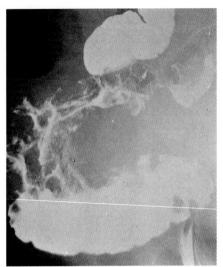

An AIDS patient complained of indigestion and 'fullness' in the upper abdomen. A barium meal was performed.
(a) What is the likely diagnosis?
(b) What other sites are commonly involved by this disease?
(c) How would you treat this man?

134

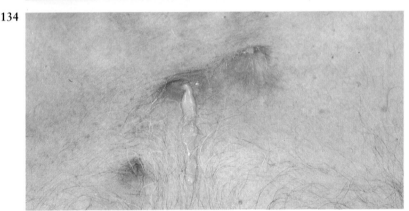

134 This 62-year-old Italian man gave a three month history of discharging fistulae from the sterno-clavicular joint, fevers, drenching night sweats and weight loss. He is shown to have an aneurysm of the ascending aorta on CT scan.
(a) What are the possible causes of the osteomyelitis?
(b) Which is most likely, given the associated intrathoracic pathology?
(c) What other investigations should be performed?

135 This is the chest radiograph of a 45-year-old Brazilian man with AIDS who was being investigated for diarrhoea and fevers of five weeks' duration. Broncho-scopy showed a few worms, approximately 3 mm in length, in the bronchi.
(a) What is the diagnosis?
(b) How might the disease present?
(c) What is the therapy?

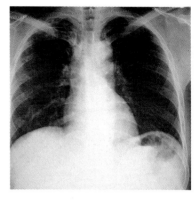

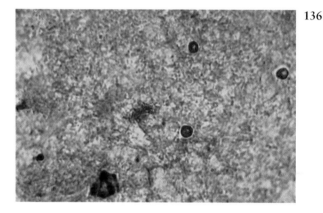

136 A 38-year-old HIV-positive man had been diagnosed with *Mycobacterium avium intracellulare* (MAI) involving the bowel three months earlier. He had shown a symptomatic response to combination therapy which included rifabutin. He presented to the hospital with a recurrence of his diarrhoea. The patient thought he had an exacerbation of his MAI, but the doctor was concerned that another bowel pathogen might be present. A Ziehl-Neelsen stained stool specimen is shown.
(a) Was the patient right?
(b) Was the doctor correct?
(c) How should this patient be treated?

137

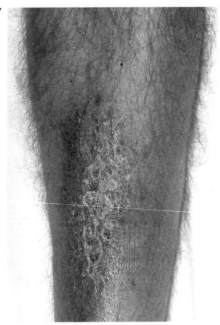

137 This patient has proven Kaposi's sarcoma (KS) of the small bowel, associated with weight loss and drenching night sweats. The lesion on his shin progressively increased in size and was shown also to be KS on biopsy.
(a) What local complications may arise?
(b) What treatments are available for KS?
(c) Which would be the most suitable form of therapy for this patient?

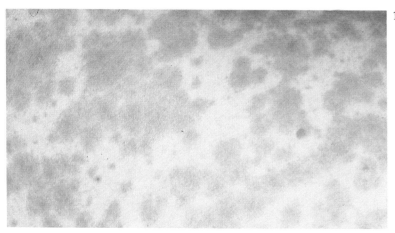

138 This patient had *Pneumocystis carinii* pneumonia (PCP) and was undergoing treatment with high-dose co-trimoxazole.
(a) What is the most likely cause of this rash?
(b) How could it be overcome?
(c) What treatments are available for PCP?

139 A 22-year-old homosexual man presented to casualty with a history of increasing shortness of breath over a few hours. There was no sputum production or chest pain. On examination he was apyrexial, with a respiratory rate of 36 per minute and expiratory wheezes throughout both lung fields.
(a) What abnormality is seen on the chest radiograph?
(b) What is the most likely diagnosis?
(c) What other diagnoses should be considered?

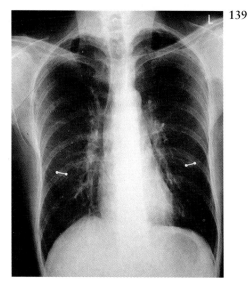

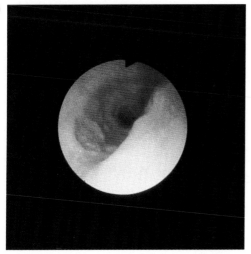

140 A patient with AIDS-related complex presented with dysphagia and was found to have oral *Candida*. The oral *Candida* was cleared using fluconazole, but the dysphagia remained. An endoscopy was performed and the appearance of the lower third of the oesophagus is shown.
(a) What is the most likely diagnosis?
(b) How should this condition be treated?
(c) Where else should one look for evidence of the disease which was responsible for the oesophageal abnormality?

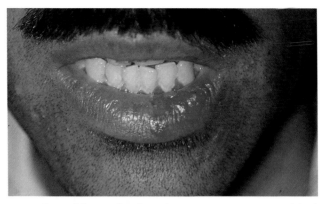

141 This cold sore developed in an AIDS patient and had been present for five weeks.
(a) What features of the lesion suggest immune deficiency?
(b) What is the treatment in this case?
(c) Will maintenance be required?

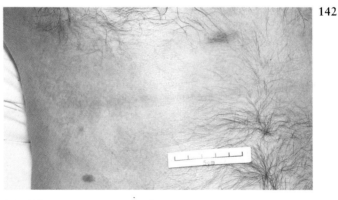

142 This atopic patient with cutaneous Kaposi's sarcoma (KS) noticed exacerbation of his long-standing skin complaint at the time of development of the KS.
(a) What is the condition?
(b) How might HIV infection have affected this condition?

143

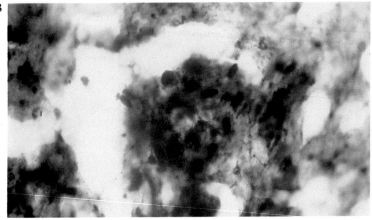

144

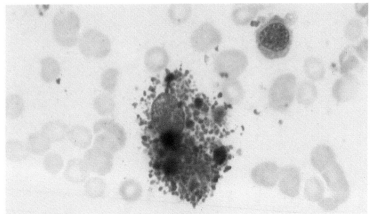

143, 144 A patient with AIDS had been undergoing treatment with the anti-HIV agent zidovudine (AZT) for two years. A bone marrow aspirate was performed as part of the investigation of a pyrexia of unknown origin. A Perl's stain (**143**) and May–Grünwald–Giemsa stain (**144**) are shown.

(a) What complication of AZT therapy has occurred?

(b) What are the other causes of this condition?

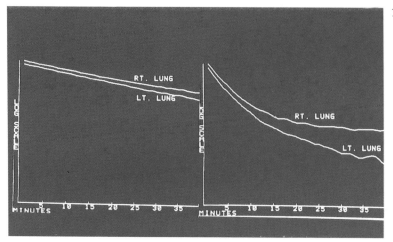

145 These are the results of a diethylenetriaminepentaacetic acid (DTPA) scan (measuring the transfer of nebulised ^{99m}Technetium DTPA from lung to blood) of a 30-year-old HIV-positive man with a two week history of cough and shortness of breath, but with a normal clinical examination and chest radiograph. A log scale of label uptake in the right and left lung fields is shown on the y-axis and time along the x-axis in the patient (right graph) compared to a healthy control (left graph).

(a) What abnormality is shown?

(b) What is the most likely diagnosis in this case and the differential?

(c) What can give false positives using this technique?

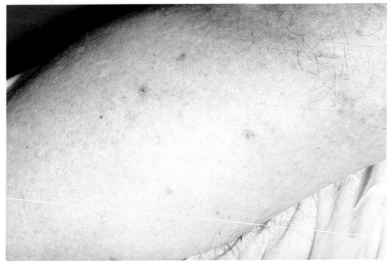

146 This patient with AIDS developed similar lesions to those shown, on the forehead, upper and lower limbs. The spots were mildly itchy and had necrotic centres.
(a) What is the most likely pathological diagnosis?
(b) What are the differential diagnoses?
(c) What would skin biopsy show?

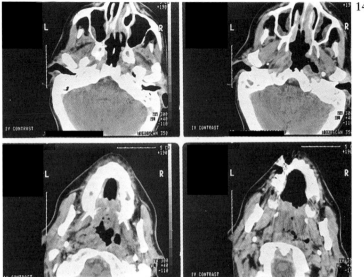

147 This Greek man with AIDS gave a four month history of severe halitosis and purulent postnasal drip, which had not responded to broad-spectrum antibiotics. Examination of the ŏropharynx initially showed a white plaque on the hard palate which increased in size and eventually eroded through.

(a) What does the CT scan show?

(b) What are the non-malignant causes of such a lesion?

(c) What are the malignant causes?

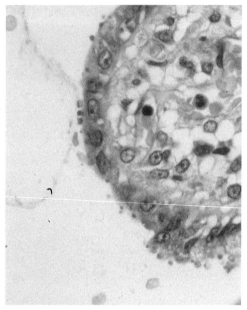

148 A patient who had had AIDS for 18 months developed increasing watery diarrhoea over the course of a month, with up to 10 litres of stool per day, nausea, vomiting and a low-grade fever. Small bowel biopsy was performed and revealed the presence of intracellular (but extracytoplasmic) protozoa along the villous brush border as shown.
(a) What is the diagnosis?
(b) Which other sites are affected by this organism and cause symptoms?
(c) What other members of this family cause bowel disease in AIDS patients?

149 An HIV-positive patient, previously asymptomatic, presented with mild dysphagia. Apart from some hairy oral leukoplakia, no abnormality was found on physical examination. Endoscopy revealed an ulcer in the mid-third of the oesophagus, which was biopsied. The patient, who was well informed, knew that one of the commonest causes of ulceration in HIV infection is herpes simplex infection, and he asked for acyclovir.

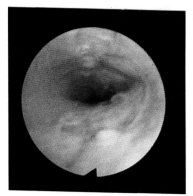

(a) Is the patient likely to be correct in his diagnosis?
(b) What other diagnoses should be considered?
(c) Did the patient ask for the correct therapy?

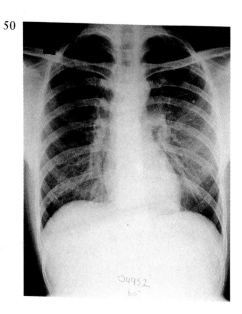

150 A 32-year-old man presented to his doctor with a two week history of increasing fevers, non-productive cough and shortness of breath. He was a non-smoker and had never travelled outside the United Kingdom. He had been found to be HIV-positive two years previously, but apart from oral *Candida* infection had been well. On examination he was pyrexial, but the chest was clear. His chest radiograph is shown.
(a) What abnormalities are present?
(b) What is the most likely diagnosis?
(c) What could have been done to reduce his chances of developing this illness?

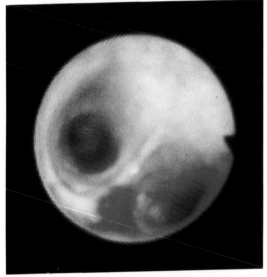

151 This AIDS patient presented with shortness of breath and underwent bronchoscopy. He had completed a course of treatment for *Pneumocystis carinii* pneumonia (PCP) six weeks previously, and had had cutaneous Kaposi's sarcoma (KS) diagnosed eight months before.
(a) What condition is shown on bronchoscopy?
(b) What complications may arise from this condition?
(c) In recent years this condition has become a more frequent cause of severe morbidity and mortality in AIDS patients. Why?

* Fig. **151** reproduced from page 954 of *Respiratory Medicine* (1990; eds Brewis, Gibson and Geddes) by kind permission of Baillière Tindall.

152 A 41-year-old HIV-positive man presented with weakness in his right arm and leg. CT scan of the brain was normal and magnetic resonance imaging (MRI) was performed.

(a) What abnormalities are seen on the MRI?

(b) What is the differential diagnosis?

(c) What should the management be?

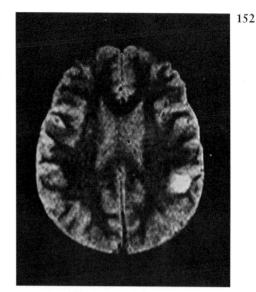

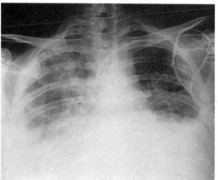

153 This AIDS patient presented with increasing shortness of breath.

(a) What is the differential diagnosis of the chest X-ray appearances in this case?

(b) What further investigations would you perform?

ANSWERS

1 (a) Hairy oral leukoplakia. This lesion involving the lateral borders of the tongue is painless and, unlike oral *Candida*, cannot be easily scraped off. The other site that may be involved is the oesophagus (typically mid-third).

(b) Histology demonstrates koilocytoid changes suggestive of wart virus infection. However, immunofluorescence and *in situ* hybridisation studies have demonstrated foci of Epstein–Barr virus-infected epithelial cells within the lesions rather than human papilloma virus. Treatment with acyclovir has been shown to be of use in some patients.

(c) Yes, this lesion at this site is highly suggestive of HIV infection. It is only very rarely found in non-HIV-related immune deficiency. It is also a prognostic sign for the development of AIDS in those who are HIV-positive, especially in conjunction with other AIDS-related complex features.

2 (a) Stevens–Johnson syndrome. This syndrome consists of cutaneous erythema multiforme with ulceration of the mouth, and occasionally the eyes, nose and genital mucosa.

(b) The most likely cause is a drug reaction. Sulphonamides are used (in combination with pyrimethamine) as first line treatment of toxoplasmosis, and these are a well-recognised cause of Stevens–Johnson syndrome.

(c) Herpes simplex infection is a cause of perioral ulceration and also may lead to Stevens–Johnson syndrome. Other causes, although less likely in this context, include Behçet's syndrome, Crohn's disease and neutropenia.

3 (a) Extensive fine ulceration with plaques can be seen in the oesophagus.

(b) These features are typical of oesophageal candidiasis.

(c) The development of unprovoked oesophageal *Candida* infection in an HIV-positive individual (i.e. in a non-diabetic, not on broad-spectrum antibiotics or systemic corticosteroids) means that the patient fulfils the criteria for the diagnosis of AIDS (CDC 4 C1). Diagnosis could be confirmed by oesophagoscopy and biopsy.

4 (a) Kaposi's sarcoma. The palate is a typical site for lesions which may be completely flat or raised as in this case. The lesions rarely erode the palate, but can involve the nasopharynx.

(b) Lymphoma; granuloma; infection: (i) fungal infection; (ii) gumma; (iii) mycobacterial infection.

(c) The presence of hairy oral leukoplakia of the tongue would be highly suggestive of HIV infection, being extremely rare in other immunodeficiency states. Oral *Candida* in a patient with no known predisposing factors is also a sign of immune deficiency, although not specific to HIV infection.

5 (a) Cytomegalovirus (CMV) retinitis. The retina shows a granular white ischaemic appearance on the temporal side of the macula. In CMV retinitis there is full thickness retinal necrosis leading to clear demarcation between normal and necrotic areas.

(b) Nasal field in the left eye. The close proximity of the area of retinitis to the macula explains the relatively sudden loss of vision. Treatment with specific anti-CMV agents (ganciclovir or foscarnet) must be started immediately in this situation to prevent further spread of the retinitis and blindness. Maintenance treatment is continued for life, as the anti-viral agents inhibit replication but do not eradicate the virus. Hence, further episodes and progressive visual loss may occur without continual therapy.

(c) Yes. If untreated, the infection usually involves the other eye, either at time of diagnosis or within the next few months. Lesions may be peripheral and asymptomatic; therefore, it is necessary to dilate the pupils and use indirect funduscopy to exclude infection. CMV retinitis is described as a wildfire retinitis as it spreads throughout the retina, destroying all in its path. Treatment should consequently be considered even in lesions distant from the macula.

6, 7 (a) Human papilloma (wart) virus. Typical raised, rough, hyperkeratotic papules.

(b) Köbner phenomenon, the development of wart lesions at the sites of needle stabs due to inoculation of virus.

(c) Yes. Cell-mediated immunity is important in the control of wart virus infection. The extent of lesions in this individual is suggestive of immune deficiency, and the most likely cause in this risk group is HIV.

8 (a) HIV-related prurigo is the most likely diagnosis. The itchy maculo-papular rash is typical and may persist for many months. No causative agent has been identified and the response to treatment with antihistamines and topical steroids is generally poor. It is common in African AIDS patients, but rarely seen in European or USA patients. Other possible diagnoses include scabies (the Norwegian variant may occur in the immunosuppressed individual), larva migrans and insect bites.

(b) Heterosexual transmission accounts for over 80% of cases of AIDS in Africa, and the male-to-female ratio is approximately 1:1.

9 (a) Abdominal lymphadenopathy, involving the para-aortic and mesenteric nodes.

(b) Mycobacterial infection (*Mycobacterium tuberculosis* – MTB – or atypical forms, usually *M. avium intracellulare*), lymphoma, Kaposi's sarcoma.

(c) Lymph node biopsy for histology and culture. In this case a tru-cut biopsy under CT scanning was performed and demonstrated numerous acid-fast bacilli which cultured as MTB. The latter is commonly one of the first infections to emerge in the patient with HIV-related disease, as it is pathogenic even in the immunocompetent host and can reactivate at a relatively early stage of immune deficiency in HIV-positive individuals. Tuberculosis is a more frequent presenting infection in African patients, where exposure to MTB is nearly universal, than in European/American patients.

10 (a) Kaposi's sarcoma (KS) is seen replacing part of the lamina propria and infiltrating between glands. This ill-defined spindle-cell lesion, with numerous small vessels and a sieve-like pattern in some areas, is typical of KS.

(b) In the bowel, KS originates in the submucosa or deep in the lamina propria in the region of the muscularis mucosae and extends upwards secondarily. Hence a shallow biopsy would be unlikely to obtain diagnostic material.

(c) Cutaneous KS is usually present when visceral KS is found. However, this is not invariably so, and isolated gastrointestinal or pulmonary KS can occur. The mouth should always be examined as the oral mucosa is the second most common site in which to find KS and is often a pointer to visceral disease.

11 (a) Guttate psoriasis. The multiple scaly, 'rain-drop' lesions are characteristic and this form of psoriasis occurs most frequently in young adults. Secondary syphilis may cause a similar but generally non-scaly rash, and typically involves the palms and soles. Syphilis serology would be positive at this stage.

(b) Yes, psoriasis generally becomes more active with HIV infection, although the commonest presentation is with typical symmetrical plaque lesions on the knees and elbows.

12 (a) This specimen of lung tissue shows caseating granulomata formation. The diagnosis is *Mycobacterium tuberculosis* (MTB); *M. avium intracellulare* infection is rarely associated with caseating granulomata.

(b) Conventional triple antituberculous therapy should be started, using, for example, isoniazid, rifampicin and either pyrazinamide or ethambutol.

(c) Following two months of triple therapy, a further seven months' treatment with isoniazid and rifampicin is recommended. Relapse of MTB is more likely in HIV-infected individuals and lifelong secondary prophylaxis with isoniazid may reduce this risk.

13 (a) Visceral leishmaniasis (kala-azar). Oval nucleated amastigotes (Leishman–Donovan bodies) are seen within the Kupffer cells of the liver.

(b) Splenomegaly, normally a cardinal feature of visceral leishmaniasis, may be absent in immunosuppressed states such as AIDS. Serological tests for leishmanial antibodies, positive in up to 95% of immunocompetent patients, are positive in only about 30% of HIV-infected individuals. This is because of the failure of patients with advanced HIV disease to respond to new antigenic stimuli. Hence the disease should be suspected in any patient with undiagnosed fevers who is from, or has visited, an area endemic for visceral leishmaniasis (such as southern Europe, the Middle East, South America, Southeast Asia, parts of India, north-east and west Africa, and the Sudan). Latent infection with leishmaniasis is likely to reactivate in patients with HIV infection as they become immunosuppressed.

(c) Pentavalent antimonials (e.g. sodium stibogluconate) are the treatment of choice. Ideally therapy should be given for several weeks beyond an apparent cure as demonstrated by the absence of parasites on bone-marrow aspirate. Amphotericin B and parenteral pentamidine are also effective in visceral leishmaniasis.

14 (a) Both scans show diffuse cerebral atrophy, which has progressed markedly over the nine month period. There is loss of white matter, leading to prominence of the sulci and expansion of the ventricles. There are no focal lesions.

(b) HIV encephalopathy is by far the most likely diagnosis in this patient. The long history of progression, and lack of focal lesions and systemic symptoms or signs, makes opportunist infection or tumour less likely. Diagnoses that should be considered comprise toxoplasmosis (can present with a diffuse encephalitis rather than the characteristic abscesses), cytomegalovirus, herpes simplex virus, and progressive multifocal leukoencephalopathy. Neurosyphilis may reactivate in HIV-infection, despite adequate initial treatment of the infection.

HIV encephalopathy is characterised by progressive confusion, ataxia, spasticity and fits, with a raised cerebrospinal fluid protein, lymphocytosis and non-specific slow waves across all leads in the electroencephalogram. On histology there are microglial nodules in both grey and white matter, and small foci of demyelination in the white matter. Microglia are of the monocyte/macrophage series and may be the target for HIV infection in the CNS.

(c) Despite loss of brain substance, treatment with the specific anti-HIV agent, zidovudine, has been associated with significant clinical improvement if used early in HIV encephalopathy, and can delay progression. This may be due to a reduction in viral antigen load as well as to the suppression of the spread of viral infection.

15 (a) Oesophageal candidiasis. Fungal hyphae and pseudohyphae are seen.

(b) He did not have dysphagia, the commonest presentation of oesophageal candidiasis, despite mucosal inflammation. Oesophageal *Candida* may present with nausea or epigastric pain or be asymptomatic.

(c) Diagnosis may be made by endoscopy or barium swallow. If oesophageal *Candida* is strongly suspected in a patient with AIDS then a trial of therapy (oral ketoconazole or fluconazole) may be used and the above investigations performed if symptoms persist.

16 (a) Kaposi's sarcoma (KS). These lesions are typical of KS, being well-demarcated and raised, with the characteristic purple colour. The lesions typically do not itch, ulcerate or bleed. They commonly increase in size over the course of months and then remain static for a

period; some may even resolve completely.

(b) The typical histology shows an intradermal nodule composed of proliferating spindle-shaped cells, forming irregular vascular clefts (which gives the tumour its characteristic colour clinically).

(c) Axillary lymphadenopathy can be seen. Thus it is likely that there is involvement of the lymph nodes by KS. (Cellulitis would be painful.)

17 (a) i) Cytomegalovirus (CMV). ii) Tuberculosis. This is unlikely to be PCP as it is very rare for patients to relapse at this late stage of therapy, having initially responded. In addition, the abnormalities on the chest radiograph do not show the typical changes of PCP (bilateral interstitial shadowing with sparing of apices and diaphragms), involving most parts of the lung field. Opportunist infections in AIDS patients are commonly multiple and therefore in this situation an additional infection is likely. Induced sputum is helpful in the diagnosis of *Pneumocystis* in some hands, but other diagnoses – including CMV and mycobacteria (tuberculosis or atypical forms) – may not be picked up.

iii) Bacterial infection is also a possibility. Patients with HIV infection have a 'functional hypogammaglobulinaemia', being unable to mount appropriate antibody responses to new infections, despite polyclonal B-cell activation and high levels of circulating antibody to previously encountered antigens. For this reason, an increased susceptibility to infection with the encapsulated organisms, pneumococcus, haemophilus, branhamella and staphylococcus, is found – particularly in children with HIV disease (in whom the antibody repertoire has not had time to develop). However, co-trimoxazole should be effective against pneumococcus and haemophilus, and the negative sputum cultures make bacterial infection less likely.

Legionella, mycoplasma and listeria are not more common in HIV-infected patients. Fungal chest infection is usually observed only in those who have been rendered neutropenic by chemotherapy or other bone marrow suppressing agents.

(b) Bronchoscopy with bronchoalveolar lavage and transbronchial biopsy, samples being sent for viral, bacterial, mycobacterial and fungal culture and direct stains, and cytology/histology. CMV may be detected after 24 hours of tissue culture by the use of monoclonal antibodies to viral antigens expressed on the infected culture cells (DEAFF test), or by the presence of typical inclusion bodies on cytology or histology. In the case described, multiple inclusion bodies

were seen on histology, and viral cultures were positive for CMV. Complete resolution of the pneumonitis occurred on treatment with the anti-CMV agent, ganciclovir.

(c) No. Short courses of methyl-prednisolone have proved useful in the treatment of acute PCP during the early stages of therapy, when patients develop what may be a hypersensitivity-type reaction due to the death of large numbers of organisms. In this situation steroids have been shown to lead to improved oxygenation, reduced fever and increased recovery rate. At a late stage of PCP, steroids are rarely indicated, as any hypersensitivity reaction should have ceased. Furthermore, their continued use could be detrimental; further suppression of the cell-mediated immune response enhances opportunist infection such as tuberculosis or CMV, and, by paralysing neutrophil function, corticosteroids increase the risk of bacterial infection.

18 (a) The retina is pale, ischaemic and necrotic with haemorrhage. The vessels are thin and ablated in the areas of inflammation, with peri-vascular sheathing. There is cloudy swelling around the active lesion and a macular 'star' due to oedema is present.

(b) Cytomegalovirus (CMV) retinitis. The choroido-retinitis with haemorrhage and ischaemic necrosis (sometimes termed the 'crumbly cheese and ketchup' or 'pizza pie' appearance) are typical of CMV disease, with peri-vascular foci of infection. This is the commonest cause of retinitis in patients with AIDS.

(c) Other conditions that should be considered in HIV-associated retinitis are toxoplasmosis, tuberculosis and syphilis, all of which reactivate with the increasing immune deficiency.

19 (a) Grossly thickened large bowel (rectal wall) with very narrow lumen.

(b) Kaposi's sarcoma (KS) and lymphoma. The thickening of the bowel wall on CT scan is much greater than would be expected with an inflammatory lesion alone. KS is most likely, but diagnosis must be made on biopsy. The obstruction has led to the symptoms of colicky pain and overflow diarrhoea. Tuberculosis may also affect the bowel leading to thickening, but the ileo-caecal area is most commonly involved, even in the immunosuppressed patient. Infections with salmonella and cryptosporidium are common and severe in AIDS patients and may be an additional cause of symptoms, but would not alone give the radiological picture shown. Inflammatory bowel disease tends to improve with HIV-related disease.

20 (a) Histoplasmosis. A sheet of inflammatory cells, predominantly macrophages, is seen. Large numbers of blue-staining intracellular organisms are present. The characteristic 'fried egg' appearance is shown where the clear halo of the capsule surrounds the organism. This is the typical histological appearance of infection with *Histoplasma capsulatum*.
(b) Although most cases of histoplasmosis originate in the central USA, especially Ohio, Kentucky and Tennessee, it is endemic in other parts of the USA, Mexico, Central and South America, Australia, the Far East and Africa.
(c) Amongst the immunocompetent most cases are asymptomatic. It may cause an acute or chronic pulmonary infection with consolidation in the former and fibrosis in the latter. Disseminated histoplasmosis usually occurs only in the immunosuppressed and may present with fever, hepatosplenomegaly or thrombocytopenic purpura, due to invasion of the spleen, liver and bone marrow. Skin involvement may be the presenting feature in someone who is fairly well, or form part of a widespread systemic involvement.

21 (a) With the history of diarrhoea related to poultry, a non-typhoid salmonella species is the most likely infecting organism (in this case *Salmonella typhimurium* was isolated). Salmonella is a facultative intracellular pathogen and is normally eradicated by the cell-mediated immune response involving T-cell activated macrophages. This response is defective in HIV infection due to loss of CD4 T-cell function, and septicaemic infection is relatively common. Other gram-negative rods, such as the *Escherichia coli* and pseudomonas species, characteristically cause septicaemia in neutropenic patients.
(b) The skin lesions are due to focal salmonella infection, the organisms being spread haematogenously.
(c) Specific therapy should be given depending on culture results. Ciprofloxacin is effective against most salmonella and could be given empirically until sensitivities are known. However, this agent should be used very cautiously in HIV-positive individuals as severe hypersensitivity reactions (some fatal) appear to be more common. Maintenance treatment is required, as the organism is not eradicated in the majority of cases, and relapse is common.

22 (a) These raised irregular lesions are typical of secondary malignant deposits in the skin. In view of the history, a likely primary site is the anus with secondary spread occurring via the lymphatics. Both anal and skin biopsies showed carcinoma.

(b) Carcinoma of the anus is well described in association with HIV infection and AIDS. However, it is not yet established whether HIV-infected patients have a higher incidence than the age-related sero-negative population. The association of wart virus (human papilloma virus) infection of the anus with anal intraepithelial neoplasia and carcinoma may prove to be important in sexually active individuals.

23, 24 (a) The main causes of hepatic failure in a patient with AIDS are infection – mycobacteria (tuberculosis or atypical), viruses (cyto-megalovirus, hepatitis B), septicaemia, or cryptosporidial cholangitis – and drugs (many patients will be on a number of potentially hepa-toxic agents, but in particular anti-TB therapy). Alcohol, and para-cetamol overdose, are other causes to be considered.

(b) Extrapulmonary pneumocystosis. The H&E-stained slide shows areas of foamy change due to macrophages laden with cysts (which do not take up the H&E stain). The Grocott stain is needed to demonstrate the typical appearance of *Pneumocystis carinii* cysts. Nebulised pentamidine is not well absorbed and therefore dissemin-ated pneumocystosis can occur, even when, as in this case, broncho-scopy fails to demonstrate organisms in the lung.

(c) Almost any site can be affected by pneumocystis including the spleen, lymph nodes, retina, kidney, skin and gastrointestinal tract. The presentation in extrapulmonary disease may be very non-specific with fever as the only symptom.

25 (a) Rifabutin. This is part of standard anti-MAI therapy and is a well-described cause of drug rashes and, less commonly, severe ana-phylactic reactions. Rifabutin is closely related in structure to rif-ampicin which can cause similar reactions.

(b) Sulphur-containing drugs, such as co-trimoxazole and sulfa-doxine/pyrimethamine, are all associated with a higher frequency of hypersensitivity reactions in HIV-positive individuals. Severe reac-tions may occur, for example Stevens–Johnson syndrome, in associ-ation with sulfadoxine/pyrimethamine. The repeated use of cipro-floxacin in HIV-positive patients is associated with anaphylaxis which, although rare, can prove fatal.

26 (a) Cerebral toxoplasmosis.

(b) *Toxoplasma gondii* typically presents with multiple ring-enhancing lesions due to abscess formation. Definitive diagnosis can only be made by biopsy, but in the presence of such characteristic lesions this is rarely necessary. Brain biopsy is a potentially hazardous procedure and in most centres would be considered only if there was no response to a trial of anti-toxoplasma therapy. Toxoplasma infection is common, with 40–80% of Europeans being infected by adulthood. Disease in AIDS patients is nearly always due to reactivation rather than acute infection. Therefore, patients will usually have a low titre of anti-toxoplasma antibodies, due to their previous exposure, but are unable to mount an IgM response or an increase in IgG levels. Negative toxoplasma serology would be against the diagnosis, suggesting that the individual had never been exposed, and reactivation unlikely.

(c) Combination therapy with a sulphonamide and pyrimethamine is the treatment of choice, with folinic acid replacement. However, patients with HIV infection have a high incidence of allergic reactions, in particular to sulpha drugs. Dapsone or clindamycin may be substituted for the sulphonamide component. Six weeks of treatment is usually given, but maintenance therapy will be required as relapse is frequent. Fitting may occur at any stage of the acute infection, or during recovery due to scarring. Therefore, anti-convulsants are commonly used prophylactically.

27, 28 (a) Myopathy secondary to AZT. This may affect up to 20% of AIDS patients on long-term treatment. The typical features of proximal muscle wasting are seen.

(b) HIV myopathy has been described before the use of AZT but is rare. This may present as a polymyositis, with inflammatory changes seen on biopsy. Other causes of myopathy do not appear to be more common in HIV infection. The generalised wasting that occurs in AIDS is distinguished from AZT myopathy which mainly affects the proximal muscles of the limbs. Myelopathy, which may occur secondary to HIV infection of the spinal cord, is usually a progressive disorder starting in the legs and accompanied by absent tendon reflexes and absent sensory level.

(c) An atrophic muscle fibre with giant abnormal mitochondria is seen next to a relatively normal fibre. These mitochondrial appearances are typical of this condition and suggest that AZT might be causing a primary disturbance of mitochondrial function. Persistently raised creatine kinase levels which appear on long-term AZT help suggest the diagnosis; CK levels fall to normal within a few weeks of stopping AZT. Electromyography may confirm a myopathy but this is often normal in the early stages of the disease.

29 (a) A severe depletion of the CD4 positive population is shown. (b) Any cause of generalised lymphopenia will lead to low CD4 numbers. Examples include the acute stages of viral infection, the use of systemic steroids, chemotherapeutic agents or anti-lymphocyte globulin and some congenital immune deficiency states, such as severe combined immune deficiency. In these situations the CD8 count will also be markedly reduced. A severe depletion of CD4 cells with relative preservation of CD8 numbers is characteristic of the immune deficiency of HIV infection (although in late stages of disease the CD8 count also drops).

In the evaluation of known HIV-infected patients the absolute CD4 count has been used in association with HIV antigen levels and clinical parameters to determine when anti-HIV agents, such as zidovudine, and pneumocystis prophylaxis therapy should be started; studies of groups of individuals have shown absolute CD4 counts below 200×10^6/ml to be associated with a high risk of developing opportunist infection.

(c) i) Gender. Females have higher absolute CD4 counts than males. ii) Pregnancy is associated with decreased CD4 values. iii) Smoking increases the total T-cell count (although CD8+ve cells are increased relatively more than CD4+ve cells). iv) CD8+ve cells fall in number with increasing age. v) Diurnal variation. Some investigators have found CD4 counts to peak in the afternoon. vi) Race. Deficiency of the CD4 antigenic determinant (epitopes), recognised by the monoclonal antibody OKT4, has been documented in black populations. Therefore, the subjects appear to have severely depleted CD4 numbers when T-cell subsets are analysed using this particular antibody. However, when an alternative antibody such as OKT4A is used (which binds to a separate epitope on the CD4 antigen which appears to be uniformly expressed), the CD4 cell numbers are normal. vii) Handling of sample. Refrigerated storage of blood for prolonged periods (e.g. overnight) leads to a reduction in measured CD4 counts.

30 (a) *Toxoplasma* and *Candida* ophthalmitis are the two most likely diagnoses.
(b) No. Although toxoplasmosis is a frequent opportunist infection

in AIDS, candidiasis in cell-mediated immune deficiency (including that due to HIV) is typically confined to muco-cutaneous sites. Disseminated infection such as this is a feature of neutropenic individuals, which was not the case in the patient described.

(c) The eye infection suggests invasive disease, most likely to be due to toxoplasmosis in an AIDS patient. A detailed history should be taken and a clinical examination made to elicit signs of infection elsewhere, and appropriate investigations performed. In this case, the patient also had right-sided pyramidal signs, a cerebral abscess was identified on a CT brain scan, and he responded clinically and radiologically to anti-toxoplasma therapy.

31 (a) Squamous cell carcinoma of the anus.

(b) Wart virus infection (condylomata acuminata); secondary syphilis (condylomata lata). The lesion is single and too extensive for these to be the most likely diagnoses.

(c) No. Squamous cell carcinoma of the anus appears not to be more prevalent in HIV-positive patients than in the age-matched HIV-negative population.

32 (a) The tri-phosphate form of acyclovir inhibits DNA synthesis. The metabolism of the drug to the active form is dependent on a specific thymidine kinase, which is encoded by the virus but not the host genome. Therefore, this agent has selective anti-HSV activity.

(b) Acyclovir resistance; secondary bacterial infection or *Candida* colonisation. In addition, there may be other opportunist infections such as cytomegalovirus or Epstein–Barr virus infection.

33 (a) Plasmacytosis. There are numerous plasma cells, characterised by a dark blue cytoplasm and a round nucleus placed at the periphery of the cell. Plasma cells normally represent only 0.1–3.5% of bone marrow cells.

(b) This finding is common in chronic infection including that due to HIV and tuberculosis, as well as inflammatory conditions such as systemic lupus erythematosis. A malignant plasmacytosis is found in multiple myeloma.

(c) The serological correlate of plasmacytosis is hypergammaglobulinaemia, and this is a characteristic feature of HIV infection. The increase is usually polyclonal.

34 (a) These radiological appearances of pulmonary nodules are

seen with fungal infection, staphylococcal abscesses, or secondary malignant deposits. The neutropenia suggests fungal infection may be the most likely cause.

(b) Percutaneous needle biopsy is the most appropriate diagnostic technique and in this case revealed candida albicans. Bronchoscopy was negative in this patient.

(c) The commonest cause of neutropenia in AIDS patients is iatrogenic. This patient was on ganciclovir as therapy for cytomegalovirus retinitis, and zidovudine. Both these drugs can cause neutropenia when used alone, but synergistically can cause profoundly lowered values. Chemotherapeutic agents used for Kaposi's sarcoma (e.g. bleomycin, vincristine, etoposide) also cause neutropenia, as can chronic use of dapsone or co-trimoxazole (used in the treatment and prophylaxis of *Pneumocystis* pneumonia) by interfering with cellular folate metabolism. Infection involving the bone marrow, in particular with *Mycobacterium avium* complex, can also lead to myelosuppression. Autoimmune neutropenia, due to circulating anti-neutrophil antibodies, has been described in patients with HIV infection.

35 (a) Kaposi's sarcoma (KS) involving the tongue.

(b) KS in the mouth may herald the development of more serious internal involvement, such as pulmonary, bowel or lymphatic KS.

(c) KS of the tongue or elsewhere in the mouth rarely requires treatment; systemic chemotherapy is not warranted and local radiotherapy is often not suitable for this region because of the mucosal damage and swelling that results. Systemic chemotherapy, when given for KS elsewhere, usually produces an excellent response in the oral lesions.

36 (a) Separate and branching hyphae are seen. The commonest type of pathogenic filamentous fungus seen in man is *Aspergillus* and the dichotomous branching is a typical feature of this genus. This organism is distinguished from *Candida* where true hyphae are rarely seen but budding yeast cells are often present. The phaeomycoses, for example mucomycosis, have smaller septate hyphae. Diagnosis of *Aspergillus* must be confirmed by culture on Sabouraud's medium.

(b) i) Neutropenia secondary to zidovudine, chemotherapy for Kaposi's sarcoma, or ganciclovir therapy for cytomegalovirus, predisposes to invasive fungal infections particularly with *Candida* and *Aspergillus*. Patients with lymphoma, an AIDS-related tumour, are also at greater risk of developing aspergillosis. ii) Conditions or treatments associated with invasive aspergillosis include chronic granulomatous disease, chronic corticosteroid use, anti-neoplastic drugs and sarcoidosis.

37, 38 (a) The development of multi-dermatomal varicella-zoster virus (VZV) is a sign of immune deficiency (in the immunocompetent, even in the elderly, VZV usually affects only one dermatome). Therefore, this patient is at risk of other opportunist conditions.
(b) The discrete painless purple lesions are clinically Kaposi's sarcoma and this was confirmed on biopsy. KS also shows a Köbner phenomenon, in this case occurring in the scars of old VZV, but also found commonly in the margins of surgical scars, at sites of allergic skin reactions, bruises, etc. The differential is of recurrent VZV, but the lack of pain or ulceration in the lesions makes this less likely.
(c) The patient also demonstrates an allergic reaction to the plaster used for dressing the skin biopsy site.

39 (a) An enlarged supraclavicular lymph node is seen. Infective causes, including tuberculosis, toxoplasmosis, syphilis and infectious mononucleosis, should be considered. Malignancies such as lymphoma and the leukaemias are possible, as are secondary deposits. Sarcoid is another possible diagnosis. Persistent generalised lymphadenopathy (PGL) was correctly considered by the doctor at this stage, despite the absence of a history of HIV, and he should be examined for lymph nodes in other sites.
(b) Lymphoma or tuberculosis is the most likely AIDS-associated diagnosis. *Mycobacterium avium intracellulare* is a possibility, but tends to occur late in the course of AIDS. Kaposi's sarcoma can involve the lymph nodes and evidence of cutaneous disease should be sought. Histoplasmosis should be considered if the patient has a history of travel to endemic areas. PGL is now no longer likely since it was established that he had had an AIDS diagnosis (*Pneumocystis carinii* pneumonia); enlarged lymph nodes due to PGL usually involute with advanced HIV disease.
(c) Lymph node biopsy should be performed. Tuberculous lymphadenopathy was diagnosed in this patient and he responded well to standard therapy.

40, 41 (a) The ultrasound demonstrates a marked increase in thickness of the gall bladder wall. This occurs in chronic cholecystitis, but in an HIV-infected patient is most likely to be due to cryptosporidiosis.

(b) The ERCP shows irregularity of the bile duct with areas of focal stricture. These features are typical of sclerosing cholangitis. In HIV infection this is most likely to be cryptosporidiosis or cytomegalovirus infection. Peri-ampullary biopsy revealed extensive cytomegalovirus infection.

42 (a) There is an aggregate of mucoid material and organisms are seen. This is cryptococcal skin disease.

(b) Cryptococcal infection is usually generalised and most commonly presents with a non-specific malaise, often even without fever. Meningism is a late finding in AIDS and it is important to try to make the diagnosis before this stage.

(c) Conditions include Kaposi's sarcoma, mycobacterial infection, visceral leishmaniasis, histoplasmosis and lymphoma.

43 (a) Thrombocytopenia. There is bleeding around the KS lesion on the palate.

(b) Active KS alone can be associated with local bleeding. However, in this case the KS would be less active following the chemotherapy. Disseminated intravascular coagulation may occur in such patients due to infection or tumour and would be a further cause of increased bleeding tendency. (The patient is unlikely to be a haemophiliac as KS is rare in this risk group.)

(c) A major side-effect of AZT is bone marrow suppression, most often causing transfusion-dependent anaemia, but also neutropenia and thrombocytopenia. Decreasing or stopping this agent allows the counts to recover. However, if possible this must be done slowly as rebound effects due to a sudden increase in viral replication, in particular encephalitis and myelitis, have been described. With vinblastine the nadir of the platelet count occurs at seven to ten days post-chemotherapy, and so in this case the thrombocytopenia should recover without any change in treatment. If recovery is slow, the AZT dose could be slowly reduced and platelet transfusions used to control bleeding. In addition, other myelosuppressive drugs, such as ganciclovir or dapsone, could be substituted with alternative agents.

44, 45 (a) Cryptococcal meningitis.

(b) It is important to recognise that cryptococcal infection in AIDS does not present with meningeal signs or symptoms until a late stage, due to the reduced inflammatory response. Even headache may be absent. Cryptococcal infection is usually generalised and the patient is lethargic and looks ill. Pulmonary involvement may occur, even to the extent of clinically and radiologically resembling *Pneumocystis carinii* pneumonia.

(c) Initial treatment can be given with intravenous fluconazole alone, but some clinicians favour adding intravenous amphotericin B. Relapses are best treated with a combination of these two drugs as the prognosis in recurrent disease is poor. Secondary prophylaxis is essential and may be given as fluconazole orally. It should be noted that resistance to fluconazole can occur, even during the first episode of cryptococcal meningitis. The addition of flucytosine does not appear to improve the outcome and toxicities include thrombocytopenia and leucopenia.

46 (a) There is marked widening of the superior mediastinum due to lymphadenopathy.

(b) The main differential diagnoses in HIV infection are mycobacterial infection, lymphoma, and Kaposi's sarcoma. Diagnoses unrelated to HIV infection which may give a similar radiological appearance include thymic tumour or cyst, retrosternal goitre, bronchogenic carcinoma and neurogenic tumours.

(c) Sputum should be sent for microscopy and culture for mycobacteria (*Mycobacterium tuberculosis* or *M. avium intracellulare*) and bronchoscopy may also be helpful in providing samples for this diagnosis. Mediastinoscopy can provide diagnostic material if these tests are negative. Ultrasound of the abdomen might show enlarged lymph nodes which could be biopsied and CT scan of the abdomen is an alternative technique for revealing these. In this patient bronchoscopy led to the diagnosis of tuberculosis.

47 (a) Molluscum contagiosum. The patient also has seborrhoeic dermatitis.

(b) Pox virus infection. This is spread by self-inoculation and from person to person. The lesions can be treated by freezing with liquid nitrogen or by enucleation and phenolisation.

(c) The site of infection should alert the clinician to possible immune deficiency. Molluscum typically is found on the trunk in immunocompetent persons. In those with HIV-related immunosuppression the lesions are on the face and rare on the trunk. The extensive nature of the lesions in this case is also highly suggestive of an impaired immune response.

48 (a) Retinal dot/blot haemorrhages and microaneurysms.

(b) Diabetic retinopathy is most likely in this case, as although similar microvascular abnormalities with microaneurysms and haemorrhages may also be seen with HIV infection alone, there are usually cotton wool spots associated. There is no evidence of cytomegalovirus choroido-retinitis or other opportunist eye infections.

(c) HIV infection *per se* does not affect diabetic control. However, episodes of infection increase insulin requirements, and the autonomic neuropathy seen in some patients with HIV disease may blunt the symptomatology of hypoglycaemia. Intravenous pentamidine, used for the treatment of *Pneumocystis carinii* pneumonia, may damage the pancreas, causing both hypo- and hyper-glycaemia.

49 (a) Monoclonal antibodies stain for both the cysts and trophozoites of PCP. In bronchoalveolar lavage there is a slightly greater yield by combining monoclonal staining with Grocott stain for *Pneumocystis*.

(b) Exercise oximetry to measure a fall in oxygen saturation is one of the most sensitive tests for early PCP, when the chest X-ray or blood gases may be normal. A lowered carbon monoxide transfer factor, especially when compared to previous values, suggests PCP. DTPA scanning in the diagnosis of PCP is discussed in the answer to question **145**. Sputum induction has been shown to be as sensitive as bronchoscopy by a few investigators, but few centres have achieved similar results; hence this technique has not replaced bronchoscopy in most hospitals.

(c) Bronchoscopy with lavage (± transbronchial biopsy) frequently reveals co-pathogens or alternative diagnoses, such as mycobacteria, fungi, bacterial pneumonias or Kaposi's sarcoma. Transbronchial biopsy performed at bronchoscopy will increase the diagnostic yield, but as there is a risk of pneumothorax this procedure is often reserved for cases which are not typical of PCP or tuberculosis. In addition, patients frequently find it important to be certain of the diagnosis, especially if they have no other AIDS-defining illness.

50, 51 (a) Persistent generalised lymphadenopathy (PGL).

(b) In **50** early PGL with lymph node hyperplasia (stage 1) is seen. HIV infects cells within the lymph node, in particular the reticular dendritic cells; this initial hyperplasia is partly due to the influx of cytotoxic CD8 lymphocytes in response to the viral infection. The germinal centre is enlarged and irregular, with large numbers of tingible body macrophages. The advanced, or depleted, stage of PGL is shown in 51. There are few cells and no identifiable germinal centres; hence the stromal component of the lymph node, mainly reticulin and vessels, is more apparent.

(c) This appearance is associated with progression to AIDS.

52 (a) A Hickman line has been inserted. This is a long line that has been tunnelled subcutaneously for some distance before insertion into a central vein.

(b) The risk of early infection of this line is much less than for a conventional central venous catheter. The patient can be shown how to administer intravenous fluids himself, hence avoiding hospital attendance and repeated venepuncture. Some catheters are buried completely under the skin; this is more cosmetically acceptable, but some patients may find them more difficult to use.

(c) Although Hickman lines may function for a year or more without complications, infection of the catheter is common. This usually necessitates removal of the catheter and insertion of a new one. However, 'line salvage', using streptokinase to dislodge fibrin clot, followed by the instillation of alcohol to sterilise the line and systemic antibiotics, may be successful in some cases. The risk of line infection is increased in AIDS patients who are neutropenic as a result of therapy with ganciclovir, zidovudine or other drugs.

53 (a) Multiple ring-enhancing lesions, characteristic of abscesses.
(b) Toxoplasmosis; *Nocardia* (patients on systemic steroids, transplant recipients, those with lymphoreticular malignancies and chronic granulomatous disease are particularly susceptible); candidiasis; tuberculosis; bacterial abscesses, e.g. staphylococci, streptococci or anaerobes, which may be seeded during the initial intense immunosuppression at the time of transplantation. The differential diagnosis in this patient with iatrogenic immunosuppression therefore covers an overlapping, but different, range of infections from those seen with HIV-related immunodeficiency, despite the cell-mediated system being affected in both cases. In particular, *Nocardia* and fungal infections, important in the differential diagnosis of cerebral abscess in the above case, are rare in AIDS patients.

(c) The diagnostic procedure would be biopsy of one of the lesions.

In this case it showed gram-variable, weakly acid-fast beaded bacilli with filamentous branching forms, typical of actinomycetes or *Nocardia*. The culture grew *N. asteroides*. Other investigations would include toxoplasma serology, as, unlike an AIDS patient, this individual may be able to mount an IgM and IgG response. Cultures from urine, throat and blood should be taken.

54 (a) The lesions are distributed with their longitudinal axes along the lines of the dermatomes.
(b) KS is typically found in the homosexual risk group (occurring in around 30%) and in heterosexual African AIDS patients. As there is also an increased risk of KS in HIV-negative homosexual men, it has been suggested that KS is associated with a sexually-transmitted co-factor. It is rare in individuals contracting HIV infection through blood products, or through the sharing of needles.
(c) KS may become more active during episodes of opportunist infection. Therefore, evidence of infection should be actively sought and symptoms should not be attributed to KS alone in such a case.

55 (a) The superficial epithelium shows changes of viral infection, with perinuclear haloes and koilocytes. There is also moderate dysplasia of some epithelial cells (AIN 2 – anal intraepithelial neoplasia grade 2).
(b) Human papilloma virus (HPV). Dysplasia is particularly associated with HPV.
(c) The subsequent development of anal carcinoma is associated with HPV infection.

56 (a) Oral ulceration may be severe in patients with HIV infection and often no cause is found. However, the differential should include: i) aphthous ulcers; ii) herpes virus infection (herpes simplex virus (HSV), cytomegalovirus (CMV), Epstein–Barr virus); iii) Coxsackie virus (Group A, herpangina, hand, foot and mouth disease); iv) Vincent's stomatitis (*Borrelia vincenti, Bacillus fusiformis*); v) syphilis; vi) Behçet's disease; vii) lymphoma/ulcerated Kaposi's sarcoma.
(b) Biopsy, for histology/electron microscopy (EM) and culture. Routine histology may show inclusions typical of HSV or CMV, or a vasculitic process. Specific immunofluorescence can be used to detect viral antigen. EM can often identify the type of virus present.
(c) Topical local anaesthetic preparations, protective carmellose gelatin paste, with or without steroid (triamcinolone), and tetra-

cycline mouth baths may be of benefit. Thalidomide, which has been shown to be of use in the ulceration of Behçet's disease, has also been reported to be of use in AIDS. However, the side-effects of this drug include peripheral neuropathy and teratogenesis. Metronidazole may be helpful if secondary infection with anaerobic bacteria occurs. The use of systemic steroids should be avoided, as the immunosuppressive effects may exacerbate underlying infection.

57 (a) There is diffuse bilateral alveolar consolidation, particularly in a perihilar distribution. These appearances are typical of severe PCP.

(b) Pulmonary oedema is the main differential diagnosis. This could be due to cardiac disease, such as myocardial infarction, or be non-cardiogenic in origin. A history of intravenous drug use should be sought as an overdose of intravenous heroin can cause pulmonary oedema.

(c) Informed patients are now presenting at an earlier stage of PCP as they become more aware of the significance of even mild respiratory symptoms. The introduction of zidovudine and prophylactic therapy for *Pneumocystis* (nebulised pentamidine, oral sulfadoxine/pyrimethamine, or dapsone and pyrimethamine) has also contributed to the marked decline in the morbidity and mortality from PCP.

58 (a) A large cavitating lesion is seen in the right mid-zone. The most likely diagnosis is pulmonary tuberculosis.

(b) The differential diagnosis includes fungal infection or pyogenic lung abscess (usually containing gram-negative organisms). In this man cavitation within a bronchogenic carcinoma should be considered.

59 (a) HIV-associated thrombocytopenia and idiopathic thrombocytopenic purpura (ITP). ITP is much commoner in females. Drug-related thrombocytopenia and acute viral infection should be considered in this case. Rarely, acute leukaemia can present with thrombocytopenia with an otherwise normal blood film.

(b) A history of any recent medication should be taken. He should be asked if there are any risk factors for HIV (e.g. homosexual intercourse, intravenous drug use, history of receiving blood products).

(c) A bone marrow should be performed: in HIV-associated thrombocytopenia and ITP this will be essentially normal, but may show increased megakaryopoiesis. Leukaemia would be shown on the bone marrow. Decreased megakaryopoiesis would be consistent with a drug or viral effect. An HIV antibody test should be offered, with counselling, if risk factors are present. If the HIV antibody test is positive then zidovudine (AZT) is the treatment of choice, as it is usually effective in raising the platelet count in cases of HIV-associated thrombocytopenia. Platelet transfusion is required only if serious haemorrhage occurs. Treatment with corticosteroids or human immunoglobulin, as used in ITP, is usually not required and the thrombocytopenia usually resolves spontaneously or with AZT. Splenectomy should be avoided in HIV-associated thrombocytopenia as this is associated with an increased risk of infection, particularly with pneumococcal septicaemia, and adds to the immunodeficiency. Partial embolisation of the splenic vessels may lead to some improvement in the thrombocytopenia while avoiding these complications.

60 (a) Numerous cytomegalovirus (CMV) infected cells showing typical inclusion bodies are seen in the sub-epithelial zone surrounded by inflammatory cells. The biopsy is of the area adjacent to the ulcer as the epithelium is intact.
(b) CMV commonly involves the retina and can also involve any part of the gastrointestinal tract including the hepatobiliary system, but with a predilection for the colon. CMV may cause a pneumonitis, although this is much less common in AIDS than in other immunosuppressed states, such as renal transplantation. Central nervous system infection with CMV may cause an encephalitis or myelitis.
(c) Treatment with ganciclovir or foscarnet is usually effective. However, these agents only suppress viral replication and do not eradicate the infection. Therefore, relapse is common.

61, 62 (a) Both endoscopies show Kaposi's sarcoma (KS) involving the stomach. The first shows early involvement with KS, with a reddened appearance of the mucosa which is still flat. The second appearance shows an advanced stage of gastric KS in which the tumour is raised and nodular.
(b) Mucosal biopsy at the early stage is unlikely to show KS because the tumour arises deep in the submucosa. Biopsy at the later stage is more likely to show KS, but a deep biopsy should still be taken.
(c) Systemic chemotherapy is usually required for KS of the bowel

using, for example, bleomycin and vincristine, vinblastine, etoposide or epirubicin.

63 (a) Glomus tumour. A tender purple papule is typical.
(b) The glomus tumour is derived from the neuromyo-arterial glomus and all three tissues are represented. Endothelial lined slits are surrounded by spherical cells with well-demarcated cell membranes and centrally placed oval vesicular nuclei ('glomus' cells, thought to be of muscle cell origin). Nerve fibres can be detected intertwining between the cells.
(c) KS lesions are usually painless.

64 (a) The maculo-papular rash is non-specific but the following should be considered in this patient: i) Penicillin allergy (as was the case in this individual). ii) Acute HIV infection/HIV-seroconversion illness. The sore throat may have been part of the 'flu-like illness that can accompany seroconversion. iii) Secondary syphilis. Syphilis should always be considered in a sexually active individual. iv) Infectious mono-nucleosis (although a rash typically occurs with ampicillin rather than penicillin).
(b) i) Take a detailed history of previous antibiotic reactions. ii) HIV antigen and antibody (IgM and IgG). In the very early stages of acute HIV infection (within one to three weeks), only HIV antigen may be detected. However, the seroconversion illness (although only occurring in approximately 10% of sexually-acquired HIV infection) usually coincides with the development of specific antibody; this condition may result from circulating immune complex formation. iii) Syphilis serology. HIV-infected individuals retain the ability to mount a VDRL (Venereal Disease Reference Laboratory) response. iv) Paul–Bunnell, Monospot, Epstein–Barr virus titres, and a throat swab for viral and bacterial culture, should also be performed.
(c) Stop the antibiotics (the timing and characteristics of the rash are not suggestive of streptococcal disease).

65 (a) Pulmonary (endobronchial) Kaposi's sarcoma (KS). The submucosa shows irregular spaces lined by prominent endothelial cells. This is typical of the 'arborising' pattern seen in KS.
(b) Most patients with pulmonary KS have cutaneous disease, although rarely this is not so, as in this case. The chest X-ray may be suggestive of the diagnosis, with patchy infiltration and pleural effusions or evidence of bronchial obstruction. Bronchoscopy may reveal

purple lesions and this is usually sufficient for a diagnosis. This case was unusual as the lesions are normally too deep for bronchoscopic biopsy. For parenchymal KS, a needle biopsy or open lung biopsy is often the only way to obtain a definite diagnosis.

(c) The main complication is repeated pyogenic chest infections, ultimately leading to the patient's death. Lobar or segmental obstruction can occur as discussed above, and also large pleural effusions may result from pleural involvement.

66 (a) In the presence of the severe oral candidiasis that is shown, oesophageal *Candida* infection would be the most likely cause of dysphagia.

(b) Topical anti-fungals alone are unlikely to improve severe *Candida* infection in the immunosuppressed patient. Therefore, systemic therapy with oral ketoconazole or fluconazole should be used. If the patient is unable to swallow, intravenous fluconazole can be used. If there is an inadequate response IV amphotericin B is of value.

(c) Cytomegalovirus ulceration is common, frequently presenting with a large single ulcer involving the lower third of the oesophagus and associated with a feeling of food sticking. Herpes simplex virus can cause a severe erosive oesophagitis with multiple ulcers; lymphoma, Kaposi's sarcoma and Epstein–Barr virus-associated oesophageal ulceration should also be excluded, although these rarely cause the severe burning dysphagia associated with *Candida* oesophagitis.

67 (a) Cotton wool spots. These are frequently found in association with HIV infection, and may resolve completely over the course of four to five weeks and re-appear at other sites at any stage.

(b) Histologically these are cytoid bodies due to oedema in the nerve fibre layer. They are also observed in patients with systemic lupus erythematosus and during interferon therapy, and are thought to be due to immune complex deposition. This may also be the pathogenic mechanism in many patients with HIV infection, in whom there are high levels of circulating immune complexes. However, HIV genomic material has been detected by *in situ* hybridisation within these lesions in some cases (but as it was also found in normal areas of retina, the significance remains uncertain). Pneumocysts have been detected in the spots in some cases of acute *Pneumocystis carinii* pneumonia.

(c) None. These lesions do not cause damage to the retina and will resolve with time. The major importance is in their differentiation from opportunist infection, in particular cytomegalovirus, which may commence with exudates or co-exist with the innocuous cotton wool spots. However, they are important as an indicator of increased risk of progression to more severe HIV-related disease.

68 (a) Several multinucleated cells are seen. The nuclei are closely apposed, and have a ground glass appearance with moulding.
(b) These appearances are typical of herpes simplex infection.
(c) Cytomegalovirus infection and aphthous ulceration. Neutropenic ulcers and syphilis must always be considered in the differential diagnosis of ulcers at this site, as should other non-HIV-related conditions, such as Behçets disease.

69, 70 (a) There is patchy consolidation at both lung apices. The close-up view shows nodularity. Radiologically this is most likely to be tuberculosis.
(b) *Pneumocystis carinii* pneumonia (PCP) should always be considered as a differential diagnosis in abnormal chest radiographs, even if the typical appearance of soft shadowing with sparing of the apices does not occur.
(c) Bronchoscopy is the investigation of choice. PCP was found as the sole pathogen. PCP affecting the upper lobes alone is rare, but is commoner in patients using nebulised pentamidine as prophylaxis for *Pneumocystis*. This is because there is a relatively poor distribution of the aerosol to the apices, allowing relapse to occur at this site.

71 (a) The barium swallow shows many linear ulcers and a more discrete ulcer near the lower end of the oesophagus. This appearance is consistent with infection with cytomegalovirus (CMV), herpes simplex or Epstein–Barr virus (EBV) ulceration.
(b) Endoscopy with biopsy is indicated. The diagnosis in this case was Epstein–Barr ulceration.
(c) Hairy leukoplakia is associated with EBV infection and may, as in this case, respond to acyclovir. Herpes simplex is also treated with acyclovir, and for CMV infection either ganciclovir or foscarnet is used.

72 (a) Lymphoma (as in this case) or Kaposi's sarcoma (KS).
(b) Unilateral lymphadenopathy with the associated systemic symptoms is highly suggestive of tumour and, in an HIV-positive

individual, KS and lymphoma are the most likely. KS may present with lymph node involvement despite the lack of cutaneous lesions. Metastases or tuberculous 'cold' abscess are also possible, but tuberculosis in the immunosuppressed is usually more widespread on presentation. It would be unusual for systemic infection with toxoplasmosis, cytomegalovirus, Epstein–Barr virus, secondary syphilis, brucella or connective tissue disorders to be associated with lymphadenopathy at only one site. Pyogenic lymphadenitis would be tender.

(c) A tissue diagnosis is essential. In this case an excision biopsy was necessary to obtain diagnostic material.

73 (a) Kaposi's sarcoma (KS) is the most likely diagnosis. This man is from a country where HIV infection is common, and he shows signs of advanced immunosuppression with severe oral candidiasis (and probable oesophageal candidiasis given the history).

(b) Immunosuppressed patients. In particular, those with HIV infection, but also a small number of patients undergoing iatrogenic immunosuppression for organ transplant, develop KS. KS is also seen rarely in patients without overt immunosuppression, occurring in non-HIV-infected individuals from central Africa and in elderly Jewish men. It has recently been shown that HIV-negative homosexual men also have an increased incidence of KS.

74 (a) The chest radiograph shows many ill-defined nodules of various sizes. In addition there is some generalised streaky linear shadowing. This appearance is very suggestive of pulmonary KS. Although nodules may be seen in pulmonary tuberculosis or fungal infection, they do not have this coarse appearance and are not associated with linear interstitial shadowing.

(b) Bronchoscopy is needed to confirm the diagnosis. Visualisation of typical red submucosal lesions is sufficient for the diagnosis of KS. Biopsy frequently fails to provide diagnostic material as pulmonary KS often lies deep in the submucosa. Some patients with parenchymal KS lack endobronchial lesions; transbronchial biopsy may provide the answer, although open lung biopsy would give the best diagnostic yield.

75 (a) Folliculitis. This often involves the beard area and may be intensely pruritic. Folliculitis is a common condition in the general population where the pathogen is usually *Staphylococcus aureus*.

The condition is even more frequent in HIV-positive individuals where it is also commonly due to fungal infection.
(b) Acne (but this would be centred on sebaceous glands, not around hair follicles); vasculitis (again this would not be around hair follicles, and is only rarely pustular).
(c) Skin biopsy would show the presence of inflammation, often with an eosinophilic infiltrate, around the hair follicles.

76 (a) The typical features of granuloma formation and caseation in mycobacterial infection in the immunocompetent host are absent. This reflects the inability of the immunodeficient host to activate the T-cell-macrophage co-operation required for granuloma formation.
(b) An atypical mycobacterium is more likely than tuberculosis in this patient; TB is a high-grade pathogen and in most patients with AIDS is due to reactivation of old infection rather than a new infection. Therefore, it would be expected to emerge early in the development of immune deficiency. Later in disease, when the patient is severely immunocompromised (as in this individual who has had AIDS for a long time and already suffered a number of opportunist infections), infection with the normally non-pathogenic mycobacteria occurs. The organisms are usually one of the *Mycobacterium avium* complex (MAC) (sometimes the alternative term MAIS is used to include *M. avium*, *M. intracellulare* and *M. scrofulaceum*), or *M. kansasii*.
(c) Infection of the bone marrow by *M. avium intracellulare* (MAI). The infection usually involves the gastrointestinal tract first, but often disseminates. The bone marrow is a common site, with hypoplastic changes on aspirate and trephine. Treatment of atypical mycobacterial infection is not fully effective in most patients. The organisms are typically resistant to conventional anti-mycobacterial drugs, but combination therapy including the investigational agent rifabutin (ansamycin, spiropiperidyl rifamycin) may partially control symptoms. Cycloserine, clofazimine and ciprofloxacin have also shown limited benefit. Drugs, lymphoma, Kaposi's sarcoma and peripheral blood cell destruction should also be considered.

77 (a) The most likely diagnosis is cerebral lymphoma (usually non-Hodgkin's of B-cell lineage). The lesion is in a relatively 'silent' part of the brain which explains why the history is short, the patient presenting acutely only because of the fits. Other conditions that are in the differential diagnosis are toxoplasmosis and cryptococcoma,

although no ring enhancement typical of an abscess is present, and there is only a single lesion – which is rare with toxoplasmosis. Tuberculoma, *Nocardia* or fungal abscesses are possible, but these conditions are relatively rare in HIV-related cell-mediated immune deficiency (although they are seen in iatrogenically immunosuppressed patients, such as those undergoing organ transplantation). Other primary central nervous system tumours are not increased in frequency. Progressive multifocal leukoencephalopathy (an infection caused by the polyoma JC virus) should also be considered; this demyelinating disorder characteristically causes focal hypodense lesions in the white matter that do not enhance, with little or no mass effect.
(b) Stereotactic brain biopsy is the only way to make a definitive diagnosis. The lesion is accessible. Lumbar puncture presents the danger of coning in a patient with intracerebral lesions, and serology/culture of the cerebrospinal fluid is rarely helpful in the diagnosis of toxoplasmosis or other intracerebral infection.
(c) While awaiting tissue diagnosis, anti-toxoplasma treatment should be started, as this is the only likely alternative diagnosis that is treatable.

78 (a) Penile warts are illustrated. Both the man and his girlfriend had warts affecting the perineum. This condition is caused by the human papilloma virus (HPV) and is a sexually-transmitted disease.
(b) Cryotherapy with liquid nitrogen is usually the favoured therapy, but laser therapy, podophyllin, trichloroacetic acid, electrocautery, surgery, interferon and 5-fluorouracil have all been used. No treatment eradicates HPV and hence recurrence can be seen with each method.
(c) HPV can cause anal intraepithelial neoplasia and carcinoma and, in females, genital dysplasia and carcinoma. The integration of DNA from HPV-16 and HPV-18 into the chromosomes of cervical cancer cells has been demonstrated.

79 (a) Multiple shallow ulcers are seen at the lower part of the oesophagus. Herpes simplex is the most likely cause. Cytomegalovirus is an uncommon pathogen in African patients with HIV infection and ulcers due to this cause are usually larger, deeper and solitary. Ulcers due to Epstein–Barr virus infection are more common in the mid-oesophagus.
(b) The confusion could be due to herpes simplex encephalitis and

the skin lesions could also be due to herpes infection. Post-mortem biopsies confirmed these diagnoses.

(c) Apart from general supportive measures specific treatment for the herpes simplex infection should be given using high dose intravenous acyclovir. It is important to consider other coexisting diagnoses in this man. HIV-related disease, such as cerebral toxoplasmosis or cryptococcal meningitis, must be looked for, and a CT scan and lumbar puncture should be performed. Non-HIV disease which must be considered in this case includes malaria and the viral haemorrhagic fevers. Tuberculosis should always be thought of as a cause of febrile illness in a patient from Africa.

80 (a) Ringworm. Tinea corporis infection. The dermatophyte infection causes this typical annular, scaly lesion with central clearing.

(b) Psoriasis (which is exacerbated by HIV infection); Kaposi's sarcoma (although the appearance is not typical, as the lesion is rather large and barely raised).

(c) Yes. The fungal infection is at an unusual site and is larger than may be expected, these atypical features suggesting an impaired immune response. The development of signs suggestive of early immune deficiency such as this often heralds more severe opportunist infections. This man developed AIDS with an episode of *Pneumocystis carinii* pneumonia during the following six months.

81 (a) The differential diagnosis on the history is one of dysphagia in an AIDS patient. Oesophageal *Candida* is the commonest cause of this symptom, but other infective causes include cytomegalovirus and herpes simplex. Epstein–Barr virus associated oesophageal ulceration is a rare cause. Kaposi's sarcoma (KS), aphthous ulceration and neutropenia-associated ulcers can all lead to dysphagia.

(b) The barium swallow shows multiple nodular filling defects and this is the appearance of oesophageal KS.

(c) This appearance is seen with submucosal metastases from, for example, malignant melanoma.

82 (a) Conditions which might give rise to facial or periorbital swelling include: nephrotic syndrome; other causes of hypoalbuminaemia, such as liver disease and protein-losing enteropathy; cardiac failure; endocrine disorders, such as hypothyroidism and Cushing's syndrome; hypersensitivity reactions to drugs, foods, wasp or bee stings; and angio-oedema. Cellulitis is an important differential diag-

nosis. Superior vena cava obstruction may give a similar appearance.
(b) Kaposi's sarcoma (KS) affecting the periorbital drainage of
lymph fluid. The lesion on the eyelid is typical of KS and periorbital
oedema is a common complication. The latter, however, often causes
diagnostic confusion, especially when it occurs in the absence of
cutaneous KS of the face.
(c) Systemic chemotherapy for KS is required. Bleomycin and vincristine were used, and the facial swelling resolved completely, although there was recurrence four months later and further treatment
was required.

83 (a) There are irregular arborising vascular channels arising from
around normal-looking dermal arterioles. These new vascular channels are dissecting the surrounding collagen.
(b) These are the features of early Kaposi's sarcoma (KS) showing
the 'premonitory' sign, and represent one of the earliest histologically diagnosable stages of this tumour.
(c) KS is commonly found anywhere in the gastrointestinal tract
(e.g. mouth, stomach, small and large bowel), the respiratory tract,
especially the lungs, and the lymphatic system. Central nervous
system involvement can occur, but is extremely rare.

84 (a) Severe ulcerative perianal herpes simplex virus (HSV) infection. The patient is known to be severely immunocompromised as
he had an AIDS diagnosis with PCP. In the immunosuppressed
host, HSV presents atypically, with extensive ulcerative lesions that
rarely show signs of healing without specific antiviral treatment
(acyclovir). Many patients do not give a history of previous episodes
of HSV and it is only when immune deficiency develops that recurrent
disease occurs. Further reactivation is almost inevitable and therefore patients are offered maintenance acyclovir treatment.
(b) Viral culture.
(c) Fungal infection, allergic contact dermatitis to suppositories/
topical applications. Although the lesions of secondary syphilis and
lichen simplex can occur at this site, the appearance shown is not
suggestive of these conditions.

85 (a) There is a cavity in the left upper zone. This appearance
suggests tuberculous cavitation. The delayed tuberculin hypersensitivity test characteristically becomes negative in HIV disease with
increasing immunodeficiency.

(b) Fungal infection is another possible diagnosis, especially if there is accompanying neutropenia,

(c) One could perform bronchoscopy, followed by X-ray guided needle aspiration if necessary. In this patient bronchoscopy and biopsy revealed *Mycobacterium tuberculosis* and *Pneumocystis carinii*, and aspirate showed invasive aspergillosis and pyogenic bacterial infection. Only when all these pathogens were treated did this man's clinical picture improve. This case stresses that more than one pathogen is commonly present at the same time in HIV disease.

86 (a) Carriage of *Staphylococcus aureus* may lead to persistent self re-infection. Therefore, attempts should be made to eradicate the organism from skin and nares by the use of antiseptic skin scrubs and antibiotic nasal cream.

(b) Complement, antibody (humoral response) and neutrophils are important in the control of extracellular pathogens such as bacteria.

(c) There is loss of CD4 'helper' T-cells, due either to the direct cytopathic effect of HIV or to destruction by cytotoxic T-cells recognising HIV-infected lymphocytes. CD4 cells activate B-cells to antibody production. Loss of these regulatory cells may therefore lead to a functional B-cell deficiency and defective humoral immunity. In addition, HIV proteins activate B-cells and these pre-activated lymphocytes appear unable to respond to new stimuli, also reducing specific antibody responses to new antigens. Autoimmune neutropenia also occurs in HIV infection.

87 (a) The sub-Saharan countries including Zaire, Zambia, Uganda, Rwanda, Kenya and Tanzania. Transmission of HIV is predominantly by heterosexual intercourse, vertically from infected mother to fetus and through the use of contaminated blood and needles.

(b) HIV-2 infection is found mainly in the West African countries, Senegal, Guinea-Bissau, Cape Verde Islands and Ivory Coast. It is related to HIV-1, having several cross-reactive antigens, and causes a similar disease.

(c) The most common presentation of African AIDS is with diarrhoeal illness, weight loss and oesophageal candidiasis. The infections that occur show a different pattern to those observed in patients from Europe and the USA, and are likely to reflect the organisms common in the environment or population. Therefore, disseminated tuberculosis is a very common early opportunist infection. Cryptococcal meningitis also appears more frequently. Cerebral toxoplasmosis and herpes virus infection also occur, although definitive diagnosis is rarely possible. Disseminated strongloidiasis is seen. In contrast, *Pneumocystis carinii* pneumonia and cytomegalovirus infection are very rare. Kaposi's sarcoma has been endemic in central Africa for many decades; however, an aggressive form was documented as emerging around the same time as the AIDS epidemic was noted in the USA.

88 (a) *Pneumocystis carinii* and cytomegalovirus (CMV). In the centre of the field there is a classical CMV inclusion cell. This is surrounded by the vacuolar foamy exudate of *P. carinii* and special stains, for example, Grocott or monoclonal antibodies, will demonstrate the cysts.
(b) When found on lung biopsy or lavage, *Pneumocystis* is considered pathogenic. CMV, on the other hand, is often thought to be nonpathogenic when found in lavage, although if inclusion bodies are seen on biopsy this is more suggestive of disease. It is often, as in this case, accompanied by another infective agent.
(c) Treat with therapy against *Pneumocystis* first. If deterioration in the patient's condition occurs, treatment for CMV (ganciclovir or foscarnet) or another co-pathogen (e.g. tuberculosis) should be considered.

89 (a) This appearance is typical of severe vulval and perineal herpes simplex infection. Extensive ulcerative lesions found in an HIV-positive individual is indicative of a severe degree of immunodeficiency and is classified as CDC Group IV disease.
(b) Other infectious causes which may give a similar appearance include lymphogranuloma venereum, chancroid or 'soft sore' (caused by *Haemophilus ducreyi*) and granuloma inguinale (seen mainly in the tropics).
(c) Swabs for microbiology and virology should be taken. Biopsy of the lesion may be helpful if there is doubt over the diagnosis or if the patient does not respond to therapy for herpes simplex. In a severe lesion like this, high dose intravenous acyclovir should be given. The dose should be reduced if there is impaired renal function and the patient must be kept well hydrated. Secondary bacterial infection is common and may need treatment. Maintenance therapy with acyclovir is advisable as relapse is common.

90 (a) No. The barium meal shows nodular filling defects in the

duodenal cap and is the appearance of Kaposi's sarcoma (KS). This patient also had cutaneous KS.
(b) Yes. Long-term corticosteroid use can exacerbate the growth of KS.
(c) Corticosteroids impair neutrophil chemotaxis and cell-mediated immunity, increasing the susceptibility to infection. However, in certain situations, such as respiratory failure secondary to *Pneumocystis carinii* pneumonia, or cerebral oedema, the use of a short course of steroids might be justified.

91 (a) The cysts of *Giardia lamblia* are seen. There is also an increased number of intra-epithelial lymphocytes and chronic inflammatory cells in the lamina propria. This is chronic intestinal giardiasis.
(b) Repeat stool examinations will usually show the trophozoites of giardia in the acute form of the disease, or cysts in the subacute or chronic form. However, as in this case, stools may be negative and duodenal aspirate or biopsy is needed for diagnosis. An enzyme-linked immunosorbent assay test, to detect antibody or antigen, is both specific and sensitive in the chronic form of the disease.
(c) Enteric protozoal pathogens, such as *G. lamblia* and *Entamoeba histolytica*, are commoner in homosexual males, regardless of HIV-antibody status, and may be transmitted sexually. *Cryptosporidium* is the commonest protozoal pathogen in AIDS, but *Isospora belli*, *Blastocystis hominis* and Microsporidia have all been associated with diarrhoea in HIV disease. Bacterial infections with *Salmonella*, *Shigella* or *Campylobacter* are more common in HIV disease. Cytomegalovirus and mycobacteria (*Mycobacterium avium intracellulare* and *M. tuberculosis*) also frequently infect the bowel in AIDS.

92 (a) Eczema. This appearance is one of discoid eczema. Eczema is associated with HIV infection and in an otherwise asymptomatic patient may herald disease progression.
(b) Mycosis fungoides. This disorder is a reticulosis that originates in the skin. In its early stages it presents as erythematous scaly patches that may resemble eczema or psoriasis. Mycosis fungoides may initially show a response to topical corticosteroids and this may be a further reason to confuse this with eczema.
(c) Skin biopsy. A diagnosis of mycosis fungoides was made and the patient showed a good response to radiotherapy.

93, 94 (a) Gastric lymphoma. This patient has a high grade B-cell

lymphoma which is seen infiltrating extensively between the glands.
(b) The lymphomas in AIDS are usually high grade B-cell, and the commonest histological types are lymphoblastic (both Burkitt and non-Burkitt-like) and immunoblastic. These forms of lymphoma constitute diagnostic criteria for AIDS in an HIV-positive individual. Although Hodgkin's disease and T-cell lymphomas also occur in HIV infection, it has yet to be established whether they are commoner than in the general population.
(c) The commonest system to be involved is the central nervous system, especially the brain, but in AIDS lymphoma also has a predilection for the gastrointestinal tract, liver, heart, lymphatic system, bone marrow and skin.

95 (a) i) Kaposi's sarcoma (KS). Although these lesions do not have the characteristic appearance of KS, atypical lesions do occur and any suspicious lesion should be biopsied. ii) Epithelioid angiomatosis is a condition distinct from KS, but associated with HIV infection. It is characterised by solitary or multiple papules and nodules made up of proliferating blood vessels and cells with epithelioid features. iii) Pyogenic granuloma. However, this condition is usually solitary and the patient normally gives a history of injury or inflammation. iv) Haemangioma.
(b) KS. These are the characteristic histological features.
(c) Yes. Radiotherapy provides effective local treatment of cutaneous and, in some cases, lymph node KS. Chemotherapy is required for systemic involvement.

96 (a) Tinea pedis ('Athlete's foot'), the diagnosis being confirmed by the examination of skin scrapings (in 10% potassium hydroxide) for the presence of typical fungal hyphae.
(b) Topical anti-fungal agents are rarely helpful in extensive disease in the immunosuppressed and systemic therapy may be required.
(c) Although tinea pedis is a very common condition in the general population, the development of severe extensive disease in an individual with HIV infection may suggest immune deficiency.

97 (a) The chest X-ray shows consolidation in the right upper lobe and the apical segment of the left lower lobe.
(b) Segmental consolidation is most commonly due to bacterial pneumonia. There is an increased incidence of bacterial infections in HIV infection, predominantly with encapsulated organisms (*Pneu-*

mococcus, Haemophilus influenza, branhamella and Staphylococcus aureus). This is likely to be due to B-cell dysfunction, secondary to the helper T-cell depletion, or to the direct effects of HIV on B-lymphocytes.

(c) One should consider obstruction of the airways by endobronchial Kaposi's sarcoma as an underlying cause of any segmental pneumonia. An atypical presentation of Pneumocystis carinii pneumonia (PCP) should be considered. Bronchoscopy revealed PCP as the sole pathogen.

98 (a) The violacious colour of this lesion is typical of Kaposi's sarcoma (KS). A pigmented naevus is another possibility; the most serious possibility would be malignant melanoma. Skin biopsy identified KS in this case.

(b) Although this condition is usually rare in HIV-negative patients, there is an increased frequency in African Negroes (it is particularly common in children, in whom it can cause widespread lymphadenopathy), and in elderly central European Jews. There have been reports of KS occurring in HIV-negative homosexual men, and this helps support the theory that a sexually acquired co-factor may be important in the development of this tumour.

(c) This condition is found most commonly in patients where HIV infection occurred as a result of sexual intercourse (either homosexual or heterosexual). KS is relatively rare in other risk groups, such as intravenous drug users or those receiving infected blood products.

99 (a) Haemophagocytosis. The cell shown is a macrophage which has ingested many mature erythrocytes (the pale cells within the cytoplasm). This is not observed in a normal marrow.

(b) Mycobacterial infection, cytomegalovirus and Epstein–Barr infection are associated with this picture. In this case disseminated tuberculosis was the cause.

(c) Pancytopenia. This may be partly due to the phagocytosis of red cells and neutrophils.

100 (a) i) Venous thrombosis. The incidence of venous thrombosis appears to be increased in HIV infection and may be associated with cytomegalovirus infection (a virus which is known to infect the vascular endothelium). Local inflammation or tumour such as KS may also cause thrombosis by irritant or compression effects. An unusual syndrome termed 'hyperalgesic pseudothrombosis' has also been documented in association with HIV infection, in which the clinical features are identical to those of venous thrombosis, but venography is normal. ii) Cellulitis. iii) Rapidly advancing KS, with extensive lymph node involvement in the groin or abdomen.

(b) Venogram/Doppler studies; blood cultures and swabs of any ulcerated areas; abdominal CT scan.

(c) The cell of origin of KS has been shown to possess surface markers characteristic of lymphatic endothelial cells. This may explain why involvement of the lymphatic system is common.

101 (a) The CT scan shows two loops of small bowel, which have grossly thickened walls, in the right side of the abdomen. This appearance would be consistent with a range of conditions, including infection, for example with cryptosporidium, or neoplasm, especially with lymphoma or KS.

(b) Biopsy of the lesion might provide a definite diagnosis, but may be difficult to obtain except at laparotomy. Barium meal and follow-through might prove helpful. Stool examination or small or large bowel biopsy might show *Cryptosporidium*. In a non-AIDS patient, bone marrow biopsy would often help in the diagnosis of lymphoma, but this is less commonly so in AIDS where lymphomas are frequently confined to one site. This lesion was due to KS and illustrates the point that KS may be very active in one site while being quiescent in others.

102 (a) The abdominal X-ray shows dilated large and small bowel with gross mucosal thickening in the large bowel. These appearances, together with the clinical presentation, suggest a colitis. The commonest cause of colitis in AIDS is due to cytomegalovirus (CMV). This diagnosis is further suggested by the marked rebound tenderness which, in CMV colitis, is often disproportionately severe compared to other signs,

(b) A similar clinical picture may occur with *Cryptosporidium*, mycobacterial disease and other enteric pathogens such as *Campylobacter*. However, most of these conditions do not usually present with a severe colitis.

(c) For suspected CMV colitis the investigation of choice is sigmoidoscopy and rectal biopsy, unless toxic megacolon is present – when there is a danger of perforation. CMV is rarely grown from stool cultures and serology is unhelpful.

103 (a) Polyoma BK virus is a cause of haematuria in this group, infecting the bladder mucosa and pelviureteric system, and may present with clot colic; bacterial or fungal infection (*Aspergillus* or *Candida* which may have seeded during the early stages of transplant when there was severe neutropenia); tumour.

(b) Polyoma is routinely diagnosed by electron microscopy as the virus cannot be cultured. *In situ* hybridisation and polymerase chain reaction techniques are also used.

(c) During the initial post-bone marrow transplant period there is severe bone marrow suppression, due to the underlying disorder or ablation therapy to eradicate tumour cells. The major infections are therefore those common to neutropenic individuals, notably with gram-negative bacteria, staphylococci, anaerobes and fungi. Later, as the bone marrow engrafts (as in this patient), the cell-mediated immune defect is more apparent (as this takes longer to recover) and infections due to organisms typical of T-cell-macrophage deficiency occur, in particular cytomegalovirus (CMV) (more common in those with GVHD) and *Pneumocystis carinii* pneumonia. The pattern of CMV in other immunosuppressed patients is different to that in AIDS, pneumonitis being common and retinitis rare, and the converse being true in the context of HIV-related immunosuppression. B-cell defects are also a late manifestation of post-bone marrow transplant immunodeficiency, infection with encapsulated organisms, especially *Pneumococcus*, being increased.

104 (a) Hypoplastic marrow. There is reduction in all the haemopoietic cell lines.

(b) Ketoconazole is the only agent not associated with pancytopenia. Both AZT and ganciclovir produce dose-dependent myelosuppression, and used together the effect is additive. Sulfadoxine/pyrimethamine is also myelosuppressive, but the addition of supplemental folinic acid may reduce this effect.

105 (a) Chloasma. The skin of the forehead is hyper-pigmented compared to that above the scalp-line. This is unlikely to be vitiligo where the skin becomes devoid of pigment. Addison's disease is associated with HIV infection (due to cytomegalovirus or mycobacterial infection of the adrenals), but patients are usually symptomatic with malaise, postural hypotension, dehydration, nausea and vomiting. Skin changes in Addison's disease are usually accompanied by pigmentation of the buccal mucosa (though this is not always seen in

HIV-positive patients).
(b) Pregnancy, menopause, with use of some photo-sensitising creams, perfumes/after-shaves.
(c) There is no known HIV association.

106 (a) The barium follow-through shows that the terminal ileum is strictured and featureless. There is separation of it from the other bowel loops, suggesting a surrounding mass. Kaposi's sarcoma (KS), cytomegalovirus (CMV), mycobacterial infection and *Cryptosporidium* must be considered with this clinical history and radiological appearance. Histology obtained at laparotomy revealed KS, CMV and *Cryptosporidium* in the same lesion.
(b) Stool examination may show *Cryptosporidium* and rectal biopsy may show CMV, *Cryptosporidium* or mycobacteria. Blood cultures may show *Mycobacterium avium intracellulare*.
(c) Crohn's disease may present the same clinical and radiological features. This condition tends to improve with HIV infection, possibly due to a loss of inflammatory response.

107 (a) The most important risk factor for HIV infection in Africa is heterosexual intercourse with an HIV-positive individual. Homosexual activity and intravenous drug use have been negligible as risk factors for HIV infection in Africa, but the use of contaminated blood products or needles has even recently been a source of risk in some countries. Spread of HIV infection from mother to baby is a major risk cause of paediatric AIDS in Africa.
(b) Some diseases, such as cytomegalovirus infection of the retina or bowel and *Pneumocystis* pneumonia, which are common manifestations of AIDS in Western countries, occur much less commonly in Africa. Tuberculous infection is more common in African patients with HIV infection. Cryptococcal infection also appears to be more common in African AIDS patients. Kaposi's sarcoma often has a more rapid and aggressive course in African AIDS patients than in their Western counterparts.
(c) The cultural differences mean that any counselling will need to be appropriate to the ethnic background. This is especially important to remember when seeing patients from Africa in a Western hospital. If possible, the clinician should seek advice and help from someone who understands the cultural background of the patient. There are of course many economic constraints which might affect management in Africa.

108 (a) Large numbers of acid-fast bacilli are seen within macrophages. This is a small non-caseating granuloma and is suggestive of *Mycobacterium avium* complex (MAC) or possibly other opportunistic mycobacteria, such as *M. kansasii*, but may also be seen with *M. tuberculosis* (MTB). MAC is more likely because of the vast numbers of organisms present. The organisms are smaller than MTB and even in this high-power film it is difficult to demarcate individual mycobacteria.

(b) Culture of the biopsy material confirmed the suspected diagnosis of *M. avium intracellulare*. Blood culture, in which the organisms are released by the lysis of the macrophages and concentrated by centrifugation, is often useful if a tissue diagnosis cannot be obtained.

(c) MAC infection generally occurs late into the diagnosis of AIDS, when there is severe immunosuppression, as compared to MTB which is a high-grade pathogen that reactivates at an early stage of immunosuppression. This specimen shows very little inflammatory reaction and is further evidence of a severe defect of the cell-mediated immune system.

109, 110 (a) Cytomegalovirus (CMV). The typical white granular perivascular exudates and haemorrhages of the necrotising retinitis are shown in **109**.

(b) Evidence of resolution of the active retinitis with less haemorrhage, leaving a pale atrophic-looking scarred retina, is shown in **110**. As the natural history of CMV retinitis is progression, the likely cause of the regression is treatment with an anti-CMV agent (in this case ganciclovir). Despite some healing of active lesions, the retina is irreversibly damaged.

(c) Rhegmatogenous retinal detachment is a recognised complication of CMV retinitis.

111 (a) This is a normal CT scan.

(b) The history is consistent with certain types of meningitis. In an HIV-infected patient from Africa the two most likely pathogens are *Cryptococcus neoformans* and tuberculosis.

(c) As there are no features of raised intracranial pressure clinically or on CT scan, the patient should have a lumbar puncture with gram, Ziehl–Neelsen (or auramine) stains and india ink examination (for the detection of bacteria, mycobacteria and cryptococcus, respectively). Cryptococcal antigen levels should be performed, likewise viral, bacterial and fungal culture, blood and cerebrospinal fluid

(CSF) glucose levels, and CSF protein. *C. neoformans* was isolated from CSF culture in this case. Cryptococcal meningitis may be associated with an encephalitis and more rarely a cryptococcoma is the cause of focal lesions. Herpes encephalitis and listeria meningitis are surprisingly rare in patients with AIDS, as is meningeal involvement with lymphoma, although these should be considered in the differential diagnosis.

112 (a) Oesophageal candidiasis. The thick, white layer covering the oesophageal mucosa indicates severe disease.
(b) This opportunistic pathogen is an AIDS indicator disease (Group IV CI), providing other predisposing factors, such as systemic steroids or immunosuppressive drugs, have been excluded. However, oesophageal candidiasis tends to occur at lesser degrees of immunosuppression than some other opportunistic infections, such as *Mycobacterium avium intracellulare* or cytomegalovirus, and hence carries a better prognosis.
(c) Systemic therapy is required, and either fluconazole or ketoconazole given orally is usually effective. Ketoconazole requires an acid medium for absorption and hence the blocking of acid production in this man by cimetidine may have led to failure of therapy. Fluconazole is less pH dependent for its absorption. Itraconazole may be used as an alternative. Local therapy with nystatin or amphotericin B may be used in conjunction with systemic therapy. If the above treatments are not successful, it is usually necessary to use intravenous amphotericin B.

113 (a) An 'owl's eye' inclusion body typical of cytomegalovirus infection is seen.
(b) CMV may also cause retinitis, and rarely pneumonitis and encephalitis or transverse/ascending myelitis. CMV adrenalitis, which may lead to Addison's disease, appears to be common. It is particularly important to examine the fundi in this patient as he may have asymptomatic retinitis, which could extend to cause sight-threatening disease if untreated.
(c) Yes. The clinical features, in particular rebound tenderness, are characteristic of CMV colitis. This in conjunction with the presence of inclusion bodies allows a diagnosis of CMV colitis to be made.

114 (a) Lymphoma (often extra-nodal in immunosuppressed patients); Kaposi's sarcoma (lesions may occasionally be ulcerated and relatively pale); secondary deposit from seminoma.

(b) Tuberculosis; cutaneous leishmaniasis; *Cryptococcus neoformans*; histoplasmosis; gumma. A travel history would be of particular relevance in this patient given his occupation.

(c) Rifampicin has anti-staphylococcal as well as some anti-tumour activity.

115 (a) Seborrhoeic dermatitis. These are the typical sites to be affected and it often also occurs behind the ears (the more greasy areas of skin are most vulnerable).

(b) Yes. Despite the common presentation of seborrhoeic dermatitis in the general population, the incidence in HIV-positive individuals is much greater. The development of this skin disease may herald disease progression.

(c) The cause of this condition is unknown. It has been suggested that it is due to a dermatophyte infection, and that the condition may result from an allergic reaction to this fungal infection. A mixture of a topical low-strength steroid cream and an anti-fungal agent is often helpful. High-strength steroids should be avoided as absorption may lead to systemic effects and further compromise the immunosuppressed patient.

116 (a) A strictured segment of the sigmoid colon is seen on the barium enema. This is likely to be due to KS involving the colon.

(b) Ulcerative colitis or lymphogranuloma venerium may give the same appearance.

(c) KS commonly involves the large bowel. The main local complications are haemorrhage and obstruction. Perforation of the bowel very rarely occurs with KS alone.

117 (a) Persistent generalised lymphadenopathy due to HIV infection (PGL, CDC group III). Non-tender symmetrical peripheral lymphadenopathy is a characteristic presentation of HIV infection. The lack of any other symptoms with such a long history makes tumour or infection less likely.

(b) At this stage the biopsy would show reactive hyperplasia, with enlargement of the germinal centres, but otherwise normal architecture. Immunohistology has shown the presence of HIV antigen within the follicles and infiltration with CD8+ve T-lymphocytes. Later in disease progression there is involution of the lymph nodes, destruction of the normal architecture and reduction in size; these are prognostic features for the development of AIDS.

(c) Tuberculosis, brucellosis, toxoplasmosis, leishmaniasis or tropical infection, e.g. filariasis (travel history is important), cytomegalovirus infection, infectious mononucleosis, syphilis, lymphoma and Kaposi's sarcoma, should all be excluded – particularly if there are systemic features or asymmetry of the lymphadenopathy. Other causes of lymphadenopathy (sarcoidosis, histiocytosis X and connective tissue disorders) are not particularly associated with HIV infection (and may be less common in HIV-infected individuals due to the inability to make an inflammatory response due to the immune deficiency), but can still occur.

118 (a) The CT scan shows low density in the white matter of the posterior parietal lobe on the right, which has not enhanced with intravenous contrast. The history and radiological appearances are compatible with either cerebral lymphoma or progressive multifocal leukoencephalopathy (PML). Cerebral lymphomas usually, but not always, enhance with contrast, whereas PML usually does not. This is a typical site for a PML lesion. PML is caused by a 'slow' virus lesion. The agent, known as JC virus, is a papovavirus.

(b) For definitive diagnosis a brain biopsy is required. However, there is both a morbidity and mortality associated with this procedure and hence the likely management value of brain biopsy needs to be assessed for each individual case.

(c) At present no specific therapy has been shown to alter the clinical course of PML.

119 (a) Perianal herpes simplex virus (HSV). Perioral, genital and perianal HSV often develop during periods of debilitation and infection, such as PCP. In homosexual men, perianal lesions are more common than penile lesions, although both can occur. The history of itching followed by pain is characteristic.

(b) Varicella zoster infection – less likely at this site and less common than HSV; pressure sores, skin infection; ulcerated Kaposi's sarcoma/lymphoma.

(c) Systemic acyclovir, either orally or intravenously, is required. Acyclovir topically is rarely sufficient to control ulcerated HSV in the immunosuppressed patient.

120 (a) There is a large right-sided pneumothorax, with a chest drain in position.

(b) Patients with *Pneumocystis carinii* pneumonia have a slightly increased risk of pneumothoraces, and a clue to the infection being present in this case is the presence of interstitial shadowing in the left lung. Bronchoscopy with lavage confirmed this diagnosis.

(c) Transbronchial biopsy is the other major cause of pneumothoraces in AIDS patients.

121 (a) The specimen shows capsulated yeast cells and hence the diagnosis is cryptococcal infection of the brain and meninges.

(b) The diagnosis is usually made by identifying the cryptococcus in cerebrospinal fluid (CSF) using the india ink stain. Measurement of cryptococcal capsular antigen titres in the CSF may be helpful as a high level indicates active disease.

(c) Following treatment with intravenous fluconazole and amphotericin B, either individually or in combination, a repeat lumbar puncture will show if therapy has been successful. The presence of cryptococcus on microscopy does not indicate active infection as dead organisms may persist after treatment and a growth on culture is required. A falling cryptococcal antigen titre (from blood or CSF) indicates a successful response to treatment.

122 (a) Ecthyma gangrenosum. These are characteristic disseminated lesions with necrotic centres. There is no pus within the lesions due to the neutropenia.

(b) *Pseudomonas aeruginosa*. Aspiration of material from the centre of these lesions yields positive cultures for the organism. The clinical features are those of gram-negative (endotoxic) septicaemic shock.

(c) Neutrophils are involved in defence against extracellular organisms and neutropenia or deficient function leads to increased susceptibility to a particular group of organisms. These are commonly gram-negative bacteria, pseudomonas, *Escherichia coli* and klebsiella, gram-positive bacteria, *Staphylococcus aureus* and *S. epidermidis*. Invasive fungal infections due to *Aspergillus* and *Candida* are also common.

This pattern of infection is different to that observed in patients with cell-mediated immune deficiency, including AIDS, where infections are predominantly with intracellular organisms due to the failure of T-cell-macrophage eradication of infected cells. The major pathogens are viruses, cytomegalovirus, herpes simplex virus, varicella-zoster virus, Epstein–Barr virus and papoviruses; mycobacteria; fungi, *Candida* (which in contrast to neutropenic states causes disease limited to mucocutaneous surfaces), crypto-coccus and histoplasma; and protozoa, *Toxoplasma* and *Cryptosporidium*. Bacterial infections in this group are mainly with the facultative intracellular organisms, such as salmonella.

123, 124 (a) Kaposi's sarcoma (KS) is the most likely diagnosis. The lesion is atypical in being flat, diffuse and lacking the normal purple hue. However, this type of lesion is not uncommon, particularly on the feet. Other less likely diagnoses are fungal infection (but there is no scaling), vasculitis, and purpura.
(b) The skin (including the scalp, genitalia and perianal areas) and buccal cavity should be carefully examined, as the presence of more typical KS lesions will commonly be found.
(c) Yes, in order to confirm the diagnosis so that appropriate treatment can be considered.

125 (a) The chest X-ray shows cardiomegaly. The main differential diagnoses lie between pericardial effusion and cardiomyopathy. Pericardial effusions in AIDS are usually caused by tuberculosis, but may be caused by Kaposi's sarcoma and lymphoma. Cardiomyopathy is associated with HIV infection and appears to be a common feature in African AIDS patients.
(b) An echocardiogram should be performed. In this case a pericardial effusion was found and an aspirate of this revealed *Mycobacterium tuberculosis*.

126 (a) Pulmonary histoplasmosis with cutaneous dissemination. Infection with *Histoplasma capsulatum* is common in the mid-west USA and, although usually asymptomatic, may cause pneumonitis in the immunocompetent individual. Severe disease and extrapulmonary dissemination may occur in cellular immune deficiency. Other mycoses may also cause disease in immunosuppressed hosts. Coccidioidomycosis is common in the south-west USA.
(b) No. Calcified lesions on a chest radiograph indicate old infection. Therefore, this is likely to be reactivation of a previous asymptomatic infection, rather than recently acquired disease.
(c) Either amphotericin B intravenously or itraconazole orally. Maintenance treatment should be given in this patient, as future reactivation is likely because of the underlying immunodeficiency.

127, 128 (a) The plain film shows a dilated loop of bowel in the mid-abdomen.
(b) The CT scan shows a loop of small bowel containing mesenteric fat. This appearance suggests intussusception.
(c) Tumour and polyps are the commonest causes of intussusception in an adult. This patient underwent surgery where the intussusception was confirmed and the cause was found to be a high-grade B-cell lymphoma.

129, 130 (a) Lymphoid interstitial pneumonitis (LIP). In neither picture is there evidence of cytomegalovirus or *Pneumocystis carinii*. Lymphocytes are seen infiltrating the alveolar walls, and a lymphoid nodule is shown in **130**, while **129** shows a peribronchial aggregate of lymphocytes with plasma cells.
(b) This condition is usually seen in children with HIV infection, where it is an indicator disease for AIDS.
(c) LIP can cause chronic and severe lung disease, and may be accompanied by enlargement of the salivary glands and generalised lymphadenopathy. The chest radiograph typically shows bilateral reticulonodular interstitial infiltrates. The use of corticosteroids has been associated with improvement in some cases.

131 (a) Shingles (varicella-zoster virus – VZV – infection). Pain, followed by a vesicular eruption, typically occurs in the dermatome supplied by a sensory nerve root ganglion. The dermatomes of the thoracic nerves and the fifth cranial nerve are the most commonly affected.
(b) The lesions are affecting more than one dermatome and are ulcerated, both features suggestive of an immune defect. In addition to HIV-related immune deficiency, patients with Hodgkin's disease and those undergoing intensive chemotherapy are susceptible to severe or disseminated disease.
(c) Yes. Electron microscopy of vesicular fluid demonstrates viral particles. Previously uninfected individuals are at risk of contracting primary VZV infection (chicken pox).

132 (a) Pyogenic granuloma. There is no association of this condition with HIV infection, but it may be confused with KS. Wart virus infection may have a similar appearance, but the typical features of the corrugated surface and thrombosed capillaries are not seen.
(b) Pyogenic granuloma is usually a solitary lesion, the hand being

the most common site (especially the fingers). The red, friable lesion with a yellow hue (hence 'pyogenic') is characteristic. There is not always a history of trauma.

(c) Cutaneous KS very rarely bleeds. However, atypical lesions do occur and biopsy of any atypical lesion should be performed to make a definitive diagnosis.

133 (a) There is gross distortion of the stomach. The antrum is narrowed and there are multiple nodular filling defects in the stomach itself. The appearances are those of advanced Kaposi's sarcoma (KS).

(b) The skin is the most common site to find KS. The gut is another system which is commonly involved by KS. Involvement of the lungs or the lymphatic system by KS is common, and often leads to severe disease.

(c) This patient needs systemic chemotherapy. KS usually shows a good initial response to this form of therapy. Combination therapy with two or more of the following agents may be used: vincristine, vinblastine, bleomycin, etoposide and epirubicin.

134 (a) Tuberculosis, *Staphylococcus aureus*, *Candida*, actinomycosis. In such long-standing osteomyelitis the picture may be complicated by super-added infection with a variety of organisms. In this case, although the underlying disease was due to TB, anaerobic streptococci were also obtained from the initial cultures and may have contributed to the infection.

(b) TB is the most likely cause of the findings, although disseminated bacterial or fungal infection may also lead to mycotic aneurysms.

(c) Investigation for suspected immunodeficiency. Even in an elderly patient disseminated TB is unusual and suggestive of an underlying immune deficiency disorder. Therefore, tumour, e.g. lymphoma, leukaemia or other malignancies, should be excluded.

135 (a) This man had pulmonary invasion with *Strongyloides stercoralis*, an infection endemic in the tropics and subtropics. Although not common in AIDS patients, it can cause more severe disease and respond less well to therapy.

(b) This parasite can complete its reproductive cycle within the host and cause disease over 30 years after initial infection. Strongyloides larvae may invade the skin (cutaneous larvae migrans) causing urticaria and intense pruritis. Bowel symptoms may be absent, but severe diarrhoea, abdominal pain and paralytic ileus occur. Pulmonary invasion may cause asthma and occasionally fatal alveolar haemorrhage. The commonest manifestations of severe infection are gram-negative septicaemia and disseminated intravascular coagulation.

(c) In severe infections fluid replacement is needed and it is important to consider, and give early treatment for, gram-negative septicaemia and disseminated intravascular coagulation. Thiabendazole and mebendazole kill adult worms, but may not be effective against the larval stage. Recurrence of infection is more likely to occur in HIV-positive individuals.

136 (a) The patient was probably correct as there is a clump of acid-fast bacilli seen, although it is difficult to be sure that this is contributing to his present symptoms. MAI cannot be cured and at best treatment may provide a temporary reduction in symptoms.

(b) Yes. Multiple pathology is common in AIDS and it is important to reassess the cause of symptoms continuously. The cysts of *Cryptosporidium* are also seen.

(c) Both these conditions respond poorly to treatment. Combinations of antimycobacterial agents, including rifabutin, cycloserine, amikacin and others, may help relieve symptoms in some. Systemic steroids may be used if the symptoms are debilitating, but their value has to be weighed against their immunosuppressive effects. No specific therapy has convincingly been shown to have any effect on cryptosporidial disease, although agents tried include spiramycin, interleukin-2 and intravenous zidovudine. Symptomatic therapy with antidiarrhoeal agents and attention to nutrition is important. Treatment with indomethacin or somatostatin may improve secretory diarrhoea.

137 (a) The lesion is beginning to ulcerate and cellulitis or osteomyelitis due to secondary bacterial infection may occur. For these reasons treatment of such a lesion would be required.

(b) KS is both radio- and chemo-sensitive. Electron-beam radiotherapy with low-depth penetration produces excellent cosmetic results in the treatment of small cutaneous KS lesions and does not further immunocompromise the patient. Intralesional chemotherapy and cryotherapy may also be used on such skin lesions. Surgical excision initially gives good cosmetic response, but tumour may develop in the scar despite complete excision, due to a Köbner phenomenon. Camouflage make-up can also be cosmetically effective for unsightly lesions. More extensive local radiotherapy would be required for this lesion. Various systemic chemotherapy regimes have been used, including vincristine, bleomycin, vinblastine, etoposide and epirubicin. Often the initial response to radiotherapy or chemotherapy is good. However, the tumour becomes less sensitive with time, possibly due to resistance combined with the increasing severity of underlying immunodeficiency. In some cases the anti-HIV agent zidovudine has led to tumour reduction. Whether this is due to a direct anti-tumour effect, or reduced immunosuppression/viral antigen load, is unknown.

(c) Chemotherapy. This patient has widespread disease involving the gut as well as the skin, and associated systemic symptoms. Therefore, systemic therapy is required. Radiotherapy could be considered in addition, for the cutaneous lesion.

138 (a) Co-trimoxazole. About 50% of HIV-positive patients treated on the high-dose regime will develop a maculo-papular rash within seven to ten days.

(b) The rash is most often due to the sulpha component of the combination therapy, which could therefore be substituted with dapsone, the dapsone/trimethoprim combination appearing to be equally effective against PCP. Alternatively, treatment could be changed to intravenous pentamidine.

(c) Co-trimoxazole, dapsone/trimethoprim and IV pentamidine as mentioned above. Nebulised pentamidine has been used for mild episodes. High-dose steroids (methylprednisolone IV) have been shown to improve oxygenation, reduce fevers and hasten recovery from PCP if used at the early stage of treatment, when some of the features of disease are thought to be due to a hypersensitivity reaction to the death of large numbers of organisms. However, steroids must be used cautiously, especially when there are coexisting opportunist infections or Kaposi's sarcoma, as these can be exacerbated by the additive immunosuppressive effects. Used in the way described above, they are a useful adjunct to therapy. Continuous positive airway pressure may have a supportive role to improve oxygenation, but has not yet been fully assessed and the potential for pneumothoraces (a feature of PCP alone) may be heightened.

139 (a) Overinflation of lung fields. Nipple studs are seen.

(b) The combination of history, examination and radiograph findings suggests acute asthma.

(c) This individual is in a risk group for HIV infection; therefore, HIV-related conditions must also be considered as an alternative or additional diagnosis. *Pneumocystis carinii* pneumonia (PCP) may cause bronchoconstriction. The very acute onset and lack of fever make this diagnosis less likely. In addition, patients with PCP often find it difficult to take a deep inspiratory breath, and as a result chest radiographs usually show underinflated lung fields. Other opportunist infections should be considered. Endobronchial Kaposi's sarcoma may cause partial airway obstruction and wheezing.

It has been suggested that atopic disease may be worsened by HIV infection, possibly due to loss of immune regulation of the IgE response.

140 (a) A solitary deep ulcer in the lower third of the oesophagus is typically due to cytomegalovirus (CMV) infection. Biopsy confirmed the diagnosis. This is not the appearance of herpes simplex ulcers, which are usually shallow and multiple.
(b) Specific therapy for CMV infection with either ganciclovir or foscarnet needs to be given. A good response to treatment is seen usually within the first three weeks. Maintenance therapy is usually required to prevent recurrence.
(c) The retinae are the most common site for disease due to CMV. Hence careful ophthalmoscopic or slit lamp microscopy examination is required and dilation of the pupils is necessary to see peripheral lesions.

141 (a) The persistence and ulceration of the lesion with no evidence of healing. This only rarely occurs in herpes simplex infection of the immunocompetent host.
(b) Systemic therapy with acyclovir will be required. Topical therapy with acyclovir cream or idoxuridine is unlikely to be sufficient.
(c) Yes. Acyclovir merely suppresses viral replication, it does not eradicate infection; the latter will recrudesce with increasing frequency as the immunodeficiency progresses if not checked.

142 (a) Eczema (atopic).
(b) Exacerbation of atopic disease has been noted with the development of immunodeficiency in HIV-infected individuals. This may be due to loss of the CD4 T-cells which normally regulate the IgE response, or due to an increase in cytokines, such as interleukin-4, that are thought to stimulate IgE production. In addition, anxiety is asso-

ciated with exacerbations of atopic eczema, and the stress of his illness may have contributed to its development.

143, 144 (a) Anaemia requiring multiple transfusion leading to 'transfusional haemosiderosis'. The Perl's stain demonstrates a marked increase in iron in the marrow (blue/black). The cell shown is a macrophage, the dark granules in the cytoplasm being iron, and demonstrates the reticulo-endothelial cell overload.
(b) Other causes of iron overload are primary haemochromatosis, alcoholic cirrhosis, excess intake (for example, using iron pots for cooking), conditions with ineffective erythropoiesis such as thalassaemia and sideroblastic anaemia.

145 (a) DTPA transfer is a measure of alveolar membrane integrity. There is an increased rate of 'leakage' of the label from both lungs in the patient with a calculated half-time transfer (T50) of approximately two minutes (control values being 60 to 70 minutes). This shows a biphasic pattern, with a fast initial T50.
(b) A biphasic rapid transfer curve indicates alveolar damage. In an HIV-positive patient with the above history, *Pneumocystis carinii* pneumonia (PCP) is the most likely cause. Other alveolopathies causing the same pattern are legionella pneumonia, interstitial lung disease and hyaline membrane disease, which are relatively rare in HIV infection. Adult respiratory distress syndrome can give the same pattern whatever the initial cause. This change is not seen in the other pneumonias common in HIV disease such as mycobacterial or pyogenic infections, where the curve is monoexponential.

Tests of pulmonary function are useful in the assessment of suspected PCP. The carbon monoxide transfer factor may also be a sensitive indicator for the alveolitis of PCP. However, smoking, intravenous drug abuse and chronic HIV infection are all associated with reduced levels, and therefore serial estimates are necessary to detect new infections. Although bronchoscopy with transbronchial biopsy and lavage has a diagnostic yield of 95% for PCP, the presence of pneumocysts does not always indicate active disease as they may persist for several weeks after treatment, and functional pulmonary tests may be useful in the diagnosis of failure to respond to treatment or early relapse.
(c) Smokers also demonstrate a fast T50, but without the biphasic pattern.

146 (a) Vasculitis. This is a relatively common manifestation of HIV infection and usually no specific cause is identified. It has been suggested that the lesions are due to HIV antigen-antibody complex deposition at times of changing antigen load, and altered immune complex solubility. It may occur on initiating treatment with the anti-HIV drug zidovudine, or conversely when reducing or stopping this.
(b) i) Other causes of vasculitis, including syphilis, subacute bacterial endocarditis, hepatitis B, *Neisseria* infection, drug reactions (penicillin, sulphonamides). (Polyarteritis nodosa, Behçet's disease, Wegener's granulomatosis, and Henoch–Schönlein purpura should be considered, but are not associated with HIV infection.) ii) Thrombocytopenia. iii) Direct skin infection by opportunist pathogens, in particular disseminated infection with *Histoplasma*. Cryptococcus may involve the skin, as rarely may *Pneumocystis* and *Toxoplasma*. However, these lesions are rather small and the necrosis is less than would be expected. iv) Scabies, but this rarely affects the head.
(c) Leukoclastic vasculitis, with neutrophil infiltrates surrounding the blood vessels.

147 (a) An irregular soft tissue mass is filling most of the nasopharyngeal space and eroding the palate. There are air spaces within the mass, suggestive of necrosis.
(b) Infections: *Aspergillus* is a possible cause in this case; mucormycosis would be unlikely as this infection is mostly seen in diabetics, alcoholics, debilitated individuals and following immunosuppression for organ transplant; tuberculosis; gumma; actinomycosis.

Inflammatory (granulomatous) conditions: lethal midline granulomatosis, Wegener's granulomatosis, and sarcoid (although these conditions are not common in AIDS patients).
(c) Lymphoma (as in this case where immunocytochemistry revealed a high-grade non-Hodgkin's lymphoma); Kaposi's sarcoma, which may present with a pale, non-pigmented appearance; nasopharyngeal carcinoma.

148 (a) Cryptosporidiosis. *Cryptosporidium* is a coccidian protozoan, which is a common pathogen in veterinary practice and has only more recently been found in human disease. It is spread by the contamination of drinking water by animal excrement or by close contact with an infected person. Electron microscopy is required for formal diagnosis. In the immunocompetent host, infection results in a self-limiting diarrhoeal illness, but in the immunosuppressed it can cause a severe cholera-like illness for which only supportive treatment can be offered.

(b) It commonly involves the biliary tree, leading to colicky right-sided upper abdominal pain, raised alkaline phosphatase and dilation of the bile duct system, which can be demonstrated with ultrasound. Cholecystography typically shows a beaded appearance to the biliary tract due to patchy inflammation. Very rarely other sites, including the lung, may be affected.

(c) *Isospora belli* is the other member of the family that characteristically causes bowel infection in immunosuppressed patients. Unlike cryptosporidiosis, this infection responds to treatment with co-trimoxazole.

149 (a) Not this time! Even though herpes simplex infection can involve any mucocutaneous surface, isolated involvement of the lower end of the oesophagus is rare.

(b) Cytomegalovirus infection is possible, although it tends to involve the lower third of the oesophagus. Aphthous ulceration, Epstein–Barr virus (EBV) associated ulceration, ulcerating lymphoma and *Candida* are other possibilities.

(c) Yes. The biopsy revealed EBV-associated oesophageal ulceration. One clue to the likely diagnosis was the presence of hairy leukoplakia in the mouth. Another was the site – oesophageal ulcers associated with EBV most commonly involve the mid-third. This condition sometimes responds to acyclovir: this patient became symptom-free within eight days and his hairy oral leukoplakia disappeared. However, EBV has not been shown to cause inflammatory or ulcerative lesions in other sites, and it has yet to be shown whether EBV is the cause of oesophageal ulcers in AIDS or is merely associated with them.

150 (a) There is a very fine bilateral perihilar infiltrate with sparing of the diaphragmatic and apical regions.

(b) *Pneumocystis carinii* pneumonia (PCP). The history, clinical and radiological findings are typical. Chest examination is often normal, and the chest radiograph may be normal or show only minor changes.

(c) Prophylaxis against PCP using nebulised pentamidine or systemic treatment with sulfadoxine/pyrimethamine, dapsone and pyrimethamine or co-trimoxazole is used in patients at risk of this infection (with a low CD4 count or having had a previous episode of PCP). The anti-HIV agent, zidovudine, reduces the risk of HIV-infected patients developing AIDS, partly by reducing the incidence of PCP.

151 (a) Endobronchial KS. The typical red haemorrhagic-looking lesion of KS is seen in the submucosa at the carina.
(b) Parenchymal involvement of the lung with KS can cause breathlessness, and obstruction of the bronchi with tumour can lead to lobar or segmental collapse. Pleural effusions are a common feature of pulmonary KS. Repeated pyogenic infections are a frequent complication of KS involving the lung and usually lead to the death of the patient.
(c) The median survival of AIDS patients has doubled in recent years, probably partly due to a combination of more effective treatment, earlier diagnosis of PCP and the introduction of zidovudine. Because of this longer survival, KS has a greater chance to spread and, among the homosexual risk group, is now the most common cause of severe disease and death.

152 (a) There is a high signal intensity lesion in the subcortical region of the left cerebral hemisphere.
(b) The differential diagnosis should include progressive multifocal leukoencephalopathy (PML), cerebral lymphoma and cerebral toxoplasmosis.
(c) Cerebral toxoplasmosis is the condition among the differential diagnoses which is most amenable to treatment, hence a trial with anti-Toxoplasma agents should be used. If there is no response, a brain biopsy can be considered to determine if a treatable lesion is present. There is a risk of complications occurring with brain biopsy, such as haemorrhage leading to hemiplegia and possible death. Hence the indications for brain biopsy should be carefully reviewed for each case. This man did have a brain biopsy. PML was found, and he deteriorated and died over the next few months. There is no good specific therapy for PML, but some cases have a slowly progressive course and support services may help keep the patient in the community.

153 (a) Large bilateral pleural effusions are present. Tuberculosis and Kaposi's sarcoma (KS) are the two main possible diagnoses. This patient had pulmonary KS.

(b) Pleural aspirate and biopsy might give material diagnostic of mycobacterial infection; it would not usually help in the diagnosis of KS. At bronchoscopy KS lesions can be visualised directly and specimens can be obtained for the microscopy and culture of TB.

INDEX